DICTIONARY OF QUR'ĀNIC TERMS AND CONCEPTS

GARLAND REFERENCE LIBRARY
OF THE HUMANITIES
(Vol. 693)

DICTIONARY OF QUR'ĀNIC TERMS AND CONCEPTS

Mustansir Mir

GARLAND PUBLISHING, INC. • NEW YORK & LONDON
1987

Library of Congress Cataloging-in-Publication Data

Mir, Mustansir, 1949–
Dictionary of Qur'ānic Terms and Concepts.

(Garland Reference Library of the Humanities;
vol. 693)
1. Koran—Dictionaries. 2. English language—
Dictionaries—Arabic. 3. Koran—Dictionaries—Arabic.
4. Arabic language—Dictionaries—English. I. Title.
II. Series: Garland Reference Library of the
Humanities; v. 693.

BP133.M57 1987 297'.122'0321 87-12103
ISBN 0-8240-8546-9 (alk. paper)

Cover design by Renata Gomes

Printed on acid-free, 250-year-life paper
Manufactured in the United States of America

For
Mustahsan, *brother and friend*

CONTENTS

ACKNOWLEDGMENTS

Professor Alford T. Welch offered very valuable critical comments, for which I am grateful. Thanks are also due to Bob Kowkabany for his help in editing the manuscript.

INTRODUCTION

Interest in Qur'ānic studies is growing in the West. There is as a result a growing need for works on various Qur'ānic subjects. The subject of Qur'ānic terms and concepts is obviously an important one. A selected number of Qur'ānic terms and concepts have been discussed in such valuable works as Toshihiko Izutsu's *God and Man in the Koran* (Tokyo, 1964) and *Ethico-Religious Concepts in the Qur'ān* (McGill, 1966), and Fazlur Rahman's *Major Themes of the Qur'ān* (Minnesota and Chicago, 1980), and the *Encyclopaedia of Islam* contains, scattered in its large volumes, a treatment of many others. But none of these works obviates the need for a volume that would offer a concise and methodical treatment of major and minor Qur'ānic terms and concepts and serve as a convenient work of reference on the subject. It is this need that the present work tries to meet. Although it is primarily intended for the general reader who is interested in Islam, more particulary in the Qur'ān, it is hoped that scholars of Qur'ānic and Islamic studies, as also students of religion in general, will find it useful.

The focus throughout the dictionary has been on the Qur'ān. That is to say, instead of reproducing details of theology and law, or historical discussions and scholarly controversies, I have concentrated on presenting Qur'ānic material and—when necessary—elucidating it. On the methodological plane, some serious problems face one who sets himself this task. For example, what is "Qur'ānic"—in the sense that it represents the presumed understanding of the original hearers of the scripture—and what is "non-Qur'ānic," i.e. later historical construction? Or should one be concerned at all with questions of original intention and initial understanding? Without going into details on these issues, I will briefly state my position with regard to them. I believe that the Qur'ān, like any other book, does have a meaning which every reader or scholar of it should, using the resources available to him, make a conscientious attempt to discover, and, when presenting it, present it as *his* understanding of the book, and do so without making too many apologies. This I have tried to do in this work. Being the complex book that it is, and employing as it does a none-too-familiar method of presentation, the Qur'ān is certainly not an easy work to handle. A meaningful presentation of Qur'ānic terms and concepts requires a careful organization of the material chosen. In many cases it also requires expository material in order to provide background and context and explain allusions and possibly obscure statements. Such material I have not hesitated to provide, though I have been guided in this by the following considerations. First, barring one or two cases where I felt the subject called for greater detail, I have kept the amount of such material to a minimum. Second, unless it was clear from the text itself, I have tried to distinguish, by providing some kind of indication, between the Qur'ānic and the explanatory material.

A number of works have aided me in acquiring a better understanding of my subject. Considering the nature and scope of this dictionary, I have not, except in a few cases, indicated my sources. This, I realize, is poor acknowledgment of my debt to those works, and so I would like to mention the ones on which I have relied most. These are four: Abū Ḥāmid al-Ghazālī's *Iḥyā' ᶜUlūm ad-Dīn* (16 vols.; Cairo, 1937–38), Shāh Walī Allāh's *Ḥujjat Allāh al-Bālighah*

(2 vols.; Cairo, n.d.), Abū l-Aᶜlā Mawdūdī's *Tafhīm al-Qur'ān* (6 vols.; Lahore, 1949–72), and Amīn Aḥsan Iṣlāḥī's *Tadabbur-i Qur'ān* (8 vols.; Lahore, 1967–80); the last two are (Urdu) Qur'ān commentaries. From these I have taken ideas and definitions, and adapted analyses and comments, and my only regret is that I had to leave out much more than I could borrow.

The following points should be noted in regard to the format and method used. (1) The material is arranged in English alphabetical order. Most of the terms and concepts are discussed under English headings, though in some cases it was necessary, and in some convenient, to present the material under Arabic headings. For the benefit of those with an Arabic or Islamic background, terms and concepts are listed in Arabic, and then reference to the appropriate English headings made. A standard system of transliteration is used for Arabic words. (2) All Arabic words and expressions, whether used in headings or in the text, are properly explained. The only two words not explained are *Ḥadīth* and *Sunnah*. *Ḥadīth*, written with a capital Ḥ, stands for the discipline or corpus of Prophetic Tradition; when written with a small ḥ, it means a particular tradition or report emanating from or concerning Muḥammad (pl. *aḥādīth*). *Sunnah* (with a capital S) refers to the normative practice of Muḥammad; the *Sunnah*—or *Ḥadīth*, which is the means for establishing the *Sunnah*—is the second most important source of Islam after the Qur'ān. (3) Cross-references are provided, and a cross-reference, even when it occurs in the body of an article, is, if important enough, also given as a *see also* entry at the end of the article. (4) In a few cases, the Arabic terms used are the ones that have become traditionally accepted, even though they do not occur in the Qur'ān (e.g. *wuḍū'*) or occur in it in a different sense (e.g. *qadhf*); these include, in one or two cases, words which for some technical reason are to be regarded as "extra-Qur'ānic," even when words from the same root and with the same basic meaning occur in the Qur'ān—e.g. *bayᶜah*, though *mubāyaᶜah* (in perfect and imperfect forms, that is) occurs in the Qur'ān). All such terms are marked with an asterisk when given at the beginning of an article. (5) The following abbreviations have been used: S. = Sūrah (a "chapter" of the Qur'ān); Ss. = Sūrahs; vs. = verse; vss. = verses.

I have given my own translation of the Qur'ānic verses cited. Biblical citations are from the Revised Standard Version.

DICTIONARY OF QUR'ĀNIC TERMS AND CONCEPTS

A

ᶜABD

In its literal sense of "slave, bondsman" *ᶜabd* (pl. *ᶜibād, ᶜabīd*) occurs in such verses as 2:178, 221 and 16:75. But its typical Qur'ānic meaning is "servant-worshipper." *ᶜAbd* in this sense is essentially a statement of man's proper role—man ought to serve and worship God, his Creator and Lord (see *rabb*)—whether or not that role is actually performed. This explains the usage in a verse like 34:13 ("Only a few of My *ᶜibād* are the grateful ones"), where *ᶜibād* includes those who perform the stated role and those who do not. It is only when he actually performs that role that man becomes an *ᶜabd* in the true sense, as in 17:65: "Indeed you [Satan] shall have no power over My *ᶜibād*" (also 15:42). David is called a "good *ᶜabd*" in 38:17, and so, in 38:30, is Solomon (see also 19:2 and 38:41).

Insofar as it is man's duty to serve God, *ᶜabd* carries ethical connotations. Occasionally, however, it is used as a value-free term. In 17:5, which alludes to Nebuchadnezzar's attack on Jerusalem (586 B.C.), the invading troops are called "Our *ᶜibād*," not because they were particularly righteous, but simply because they served as an instrument for executing a certain divine scheme.

See also: RABB; SLAVERY; WORSHIP.

ABLUTION

Arabic: **wuḍū'*.

5:6 makes ablution a prerequisite to *ṣalāt* (*q.v.*), describing the form and significance of ablution.

I. Form. Ablution consists of the following: (a) washing of the face; (b) washing of the arms up to the elbows; (c) wiping the head; (d) washing of the feet up to the ankles. Elucidating this injunction, *Ḥadīth* includes under (a) rinsing of the mouth and clearing of the nose, and under (c) wiping of the inside and outside of the ears. First, however, the hands should be washed (another *Ḥadīth* prescription) so that ablution is performed with clean hands.

In certain situations one may perform dry ablution (*q.v.*).

II. Significance. The injunction of ablution, 5:6 says, is not meant to be a hardship; it is, rather, a blessing, and it has a twofold significance. First, it makes for purification. The reference, apparently, is to bodily purification, but spiritual purification is doubtless implied, for ablution is a means to *ṣalāt*, an act of worship that is spiritual in character. Second, ablution represents, together with bathing (*q.v.*) and dry ablution, the completion of God's blessing upon Muslims so that they will be grateful to God. With these injunctions, that is to say, the divine dispensation with regard to purification was made complete.

See also: BATHING; DRY ABLUTION; IMPURITY.

ABLUTION, DRY See DRY ABLUTION

ABROGATION

Arabic: *naskh*.

I. Meaning. "Abrogation" is the repealing of a text. 2:106 says: "Any verse that We abrogate or cause to be forgotten We replace with another that is either better than it or is comparable to it. Do you not know that God has power over everything?" That 2:106 refers to the abrogation of injunctions found in pre-Islamic scriptures is made clear by the immediately preceding verse ("Those from among the People of the Book [*q.v.*] who have disbelieved do not want, nor do the Idolators [see *idolatry*], that any good be sent down upon you from your Lord. God, however, singles out for His mercy whomever He likes; God is extremely bounteous"), and by the concluding words of 2:106 itself ("Do you not know that it is God to Whom belongs the sovereignty of the heavens and the earth?"). Thus, to the criticism made by the People of the Book—that it is inexplicable that the Qur'ān, presented as a revealed book, should abrogate the injunctions of a previously revealed book, the Bible—2:106 responds by saying that, in abrogating some of the Biblical injunctions, the Qur'ān offers others that are either better than them or at least comparable to them, the concluding part of 2:106 adding by way of comment that God, Who is Almighty, has the power to do everything (see also 2:107). The context of 2:106 becomes even more clear when 2:104–121 are read as an integrated unit.

Besides "that which We abrogate" (*naskh*), another expression in the verse needs attention: "that which We cause to be forgotten" (*insā'*). *Insā'*, the Qur'ān seems to suggest, takes place in accordance with a certain law of God (see *sunnah of God*), namely, that those who seek misguidance (*q.v.*) are misguided by God. In other words, if a people neglects the verses of God, then God causes it to forget those verses. For practical purposes, *insā'* may be subsumed under *naskh*.

II. Abrogation of Qur'ānic Injunctions. Although the word *naskh* in 2:106 refers to the abrogation, by means of the Qur'ān, of injunctions found in earlier scriptures, Qur'ānic injunctions themselves may be abrogated, as has happened in a few cases. An example of this abrogation is 24:2, which abrogates the punishment of adultery (*q.v.*) stated in 4:15–16. A study of the Qur'ān shows, first, that only a limited number of Qur'ānic verses have been abrogated, and, second, that the abrogation pertains to legal and practical matters only, and not to matters of doctrine and belief.

See also: QUR'ĀN.

ACCOUNTABILITY

Arabic: *ḥisāb.*

According to a large number of Qur'ānic verses, man will be held responsible for his actions on earth. For example, 102:8, referring to the hereafter (*q.v.*), says: "Then on that day you shall be questioned about the blessings." And 75:36 says: "Does man think that he will be allowed to go scot-free?" The Arabic word for "scot-free" is *sudan,* which is used of camels that have been left free to roam around and graze and drink unchecked. The verse is saying that man shall not be allowed to live like an irresponsible creature, but will be held answerable for his conduct.

The idea of accountability is thus predicated on the principle that privilege entails responsibility. In His mercy and kindness, God has granted man countless blessings, and it stands to reason that He should one day hold man accountable for the way in which he has received those blessings. Or one can say that accountability represents the point of convergence between God's mercy and justice: being merciful, God has made man the recipient of His bounty; being just, He will call man to account for the way in which he has responded to His bounty.

See also: HEREAFTER, THE; PUNISHMENT; RECOMPENSE; REWARD; TRIAL.

ACCURSED TREE, THE

Arabic: *ash-shajarah al-malᶜūnah.*

The reference in 17:60 is to the zaqqūm tree, which is

called accursed because, having been created for the people of hell, it does not represent God's mercy. The tree is described in 37:62–66 (see also 44:43–46; 56:51–56) in these words: "Is this [reward for the people of paradise] a better feast or [is] the zaqqūm tree [better, meant as it is for the people of hell]? We have made it [zaqqūm] an ordeal [see below] for the iniquitous. It is a tree that sprouts from the very core of hell. Its spathes make it out to be [so many] heads of devils. They [disbelievers] are going to eat of it, and shall have to fill their bellies with it. Then, on top of it, they shall have a drink of boiling water." The fruit of the tree, according to 44:43–46 and 56:51–55, has this property that it will make those who eat of it very thirsty, and they will feel as if they have boiling water in their stomachs. But, when they ask for water to quench their thirst, they will be served boiling water.

In what sense is the zaqqūm tree called (37:63) an ordeal? According to commentators, when the Qur'ān described the tree, the disbelievers ridiculed the idea. "What," they said, "shall a tree grow in the fire of hell? And will there be water in hell, too?" The Qur'ānic description thus became an "ordeal" for them in that it put them to the test of belief, a test in which they failed and, as a result, became even more misguided. The Arabic word used for "ordeal" is *fitnah* (*q.v.*), which is significant because it refers to their "trial" in this world and also to their "suffering" in hell.

ᶜADHĀB See PUNISHMENT

ᶜADL See JUSTICE

ADULTERY

Arabic: *zinā*.

Zinā is "illicit sexual intercourse." The distinction between "adultery" and "fornication" is not made in the Qur'ān, though, for purposes of translation, "adultery" may be used as the equivalent of the Arabic word.

Zinā is a punishable offense. 24:2 lays down the punishment: a hundred lashes. The verse does not make a distinction between a married and an unmarried person, though in traditional Islamic law the said punishment is, on the authority of *Ḥadīth*, given to an unmarried person, the punishment for a married adulterer being stoning to death.

The Qur'ān not only prohibits *zinā*, it also forbids one to "get close" to it (17:32), that is, to do anything that might lead one to it. A Muslim is forbidden to marry a *zānī* or *zāniyah* (active participles, masc. and fem. respectively, from *zinā*; 24:3).

See also: CHASTITY; FALSE ALLEGATION OF UNCHASTITY; IMMORALITY.

AGE OF IGNORANCE, THE

Arabic: *jāhiliyyah*.

Jāhiliyyah is the name of the "dark" or "unenlightened" age in the history of Arabia before the advent of Islam. The word is usually rendered as the "Age of Ignorance," though the Qur'ānic usage has a vaster semantic field. 3:154 terms mistaken notions about God "conjectures of *Jāhiliyyah*." In 5:50 *Jāhiliyyah* is an antonym of "divine revelation," mentioned in the preceding verse. The expression "to decide in accordance with *Jāhiliyyah*" in 5:50 thus means: to decide in accordance with the laws, customs, and practices of *Jāhiliyyah* instead of the injunctions of divine revelation. In 33:33, women's display of their beauty and ornaments is called the "display of *Jāhiliyyah*." In 48:26 "fierce attachment to *Jāhiliyyah*" stands for the unreasonable and provocative acts of the Quraysh on the occasion of the Pact of Ḥudaybiyyah (628). In Qur'ānic usage, one can see, the word covers "ignorance" of many types,

Jāhiliyyah representing any system of life, behavior, or attitude that is uninformed by the proper ethical-intellectual vision—according to the Qur'ān, the Islamic ethical-intellectual vision.

See also: OSTENTATION.

ᶜAHD See COVENANT

AHL ADH-DHIKR See REMEMBRANCE

AHL AL-KITĀB See PEOPLE OF THE BOOK, THE

AḤZĀB See CONFEDERATES, THE

AJAL See APPOINTED TIME, THE

ĀKHIRAH See HEREAFTER, THE

ALLĀH

I. Name. Composed of the definite article *al* and *ilāh* ("god"), "Allāh" is the personal name of God, and is the word with the highest frequency in the Qur'ān. Unlike "God," It has no plural or feminine form, thus having the One God as its unambiguous referent. In this work "Allāh" and "God" are used interchangeably.

II. Being and Attributes. The Qur'ān does not say much about the Being or Essence of God, for it considers it to be beyond human comprehension. That is why a number of verses describe Allāh in such terms as: "Nothing is like Him" (42:11), and "Eyes cannot perceive Him" (6:103). But the Qur'ān does say a great deal about how God relates to the universe and, in particular, to man. For while man cannot fully comprehend the "essential" aspect of the deity of Allāh, he can have a fairly good understanding of its "relational" aspect, which has a direct bearing on the universe and on man's life. This relational aspect is elucidated in the Qur'ān with reference to the attributes of God—which are called *al-asmā' al-ḥusnā*, "the most beautiful names of God" (7:180; 17:110; 20:8; 59:24)—and the following classification of those attributes gives an idea of their range.

1. Allāh is eternal, precedes all existence, and is the cause of all existence, which is contingent upon Him: *awwal* ("First"), *ākhir* ("Last"); *wārith* ("Heir," that is, He will survive all); *ḥayy* ("Living," that is, One Who is Self-Existing and will never die), *qayyūm* ("Self-Existing"; "Sustainer" [of others]); *khāliq* ("Creator"); *badī*^{c} ("Originator").

2. He is absolutely one and has no associates: *wāḥid* ("One"); *aḥad* ("Absolutely One").

3. He is majestic, holy, and sovereign: ^{c}*alī* ("Exalted"); ^{c}*aẓīm* ("Magnificent"); *kabīr* ("Great"); *mutakabbir* ("Lofty"); *wāsi*^{c} ("Comprehensive, Liberal"); *karīm* "(Noble"); *dhū l-jalāl wa l-ikrām* ("Majestic and Noble"); *quddūs* ("Very Holy"); *ḥamīd* ("Praiseworthy"); *majīd* ("Glorious"); *malik* ("King"); *mālik al-mulk* ("Possessor of Dominion").

4. He provides for all: *rabb* ("Sustainer-Lord"), *rāziq*, ("Provider"), *razzāq* ("Great Provider"); *ghanī* ("Rich"); *wahhāb* ("Great Giver").

5. He is merciful, kind, forgiving, patient: *raḥmān* ("Most Compassionate"), *raḥīm* ("Ever-Merciful"); *wadūd* ("Very Loving"); *salām* ("[Source of] Peace") *ghafūr* ("Very Forgiving"); *ghaffār* ("Most Forgiving"); ^{c}*afuww* ("Pardoner"); *tawwāb* ("Most Accepting of Repentance"); *ṣabbār* ("Most Patient").

6. He is omniscient: ^{c}*ālim* ("Knowledgeable"), ^{c}*alīm*, ("Very Knowledgeable"), ^{c}*allām*, ("All-Knowing"); *khabīr* ("Aware"); *samī*^{c} (Listener); *baṣīr* ("Watchful"); *shahīd* ("Witness"). The *ẓāhir* ("Outward") and *bāṭin* ("Inward") of 57:3 also refer to God's omniscience, for they simply mean that God knows everything "inside out."

7. He is powerful and resourceful: *qādir* ("Powerful"), *qadīr* ("Very Powerful"), *qawī* ("Strong"), *ᶜazīz* ("Strong, Mighty"); *qāhir* ("Dominant"); *qahhār* ("Most Dominant"); *laṭīf* ("Subtle").

8. He is wise and just: *ḥakīm* ("Wise"); *khayr al-ḥākimīn* ("Best of Judges"); *ḥasīb* ("Reckoner"); *dhū ntiqām* ("Avenger"); *sarīᶜ al-ḥisāb* ("Swift Reckoner").

9. He guides, helps, and supports: *hādī* ("Guide"); *walī* ("Friend"); *wakīl* ("Guardian"); *ṣamad* ("Support"); *muhaymin* ("Protector"). He is "the Light of the heavens and the earth" (24:35), that is, He is the source of all knowledge and enlightenment.

III. Analysis. An analysis of these attributes and other relevant data will show that the Qur'ānic concept of God is composed of several notions.

First, the Qur'ān lays great emphasis on the unity of God. Had there been more than one God, there would have been chaos in the universe (21:22). The argument here is that the different parts of the universe are knit together in a harmony that can be satisfactorily explained only on the assumption of the existence of one God. The universality and stability of the laws of nature are a proof that the same God rules the earth and also the most distant parts of the universe (see also 43:84). The Qur'ān thus rejects idolatory, Arabian or any other. At the same time, it rejects Christian trinitarianism (4:171; 5:73). Man needs no intermediaries to establish a relationship with God.

Second, besides being the only Creator, Allāh is the only Sovereign there is: "Lo! His is the creation and the command" (7:54). The word "Islam" (*q.v.*) means "submission," and the notion of submission to Allāh is the essence of Islam. The Qur'ān's demand of man is that he recognize Allāh as the only and absolute sovereign and live his entire life in compliance with His commandments.

Third, the Qur'ān presents Allāh essentially as a merciful God, and not as a God of wrath. In fact, the attribute of *ar-raḥmān* ("the Most Compassionate One") is used in the Qur'ān as a personal names of God (e.g. 13:30; 17:110; 19:18; 20:5).

Fourth, the God of the Qur'ān is not far removed from the world but is actively involved in it. He takes provident care of the universe. In particular, He provides man with material and spiritual sustenance. His greatest blessing on man is that He guides him and shows him the right way to live his life.

Fifth, God deals with the world and man not in an arbitray or capricious manner, but in accordance with a clearly enunciated set of principles. It would therefore be a mistake to identify the God of Islam with the impersonal Time as the controller of events. Time, as conceived by the pagans of Arabia, was a capricious and lawless force, whereas the God of the Qur'ān is fair and just.

Sixth, Allāh is the Supreme Judge, and will judge men in the hereafter (*q.v.*), meting out reward and punishment.

Seventh, Islamic monotheism is very closely connected with social humanism. At the same time that it maintains the unity of God, the Qur'ān maintains the unity of mankind: the same God is the Creator of all humanity.

IV. Are God's Mercy and Justice in Conflict? Two important questions arise about the Qur'ānic concept of Allāh: What is the relationship between God's mercy and justice? And, Does the power of Allāh leave any room for human freedom? Here we will discuss the first of these questions; for a treatment of the second question, see *freewill and determinism*.

The Qur'ān does not see a conflict between God's mercy and His justice. Rather, the justice of God is seen as a manifestation of His mercy. The point is well brought out by 6:12: "He has imposed mercy upon Himself; He will assemble you on the Day of Resurrection." According to this verse, if God were not to bring about a Day of Judgment, it would imply that, in His eyes, good and evil are the same, justice and injustice have the same value, and existence is devoid of moral meaning. It is thus a logical corollary of God's being merciful that He should bring about a Day of Reckoning. Also, if God were to invert the principle of justice, thus rewarding the wicked and punishing the righteous, no one could stop His hand. It is out of mercy, then, that He has bound Himself to the law of administering justice.

See also: ANGEL; HEREAFTER, THE; MONOTHEISM: PROPHECY; PROPHET.

AMĀNAH See TRUST

AMR BI L-MA^{c}RŪF WA N-NAHY ^{c}AN AL-MUNKAR, AL- See ENJOINING GOOD AND FORBIDDING EVIL

ANCIENT HOUSE, THE

Arabic: *al-bayt al-^{c}atīq.*

The Ka^{c}bah (*q.v.*) is so called in 22:29, 33. The Ka^{c}bah is "ancient" because it was the first structure built for the worship of the One God (3:96), built as it was by Abraham and Ishmael (2:127).

The Arabic word used for "ancient" in the phrase is *^{c}atīq,* which carries the connotations of purity, excellence, and preciousness; it is used of good wine, a good horse, and a nicely-made garment. The use of this word, instead of some such word as *qadīm,* thus probably contains a censure of the paganization of the rites of pilgrimage (*q.v.*) by the Arabs in pre-Islamic times, and an exhortation to the Arabs to perform the "pure" rites of pilgrimage.

See also: KA^{c}BAH; SACRED MOSQUE, THE.

ANFĀL See SPOILS

ANGEL

Arabic: *malak* (pl. *malā'ikah*).

A member of an order of creation whose essential constitutive element is believed to be light.

I. Nature and Functions. According to the Qur'ān, angels are not simply abstractions but personal beings: they have wings (35:1) and can assume human form (51:24–27). They are thinking, rational beings—they were curious to learn about the purpose of man's creation (2:30). They possess freedom of the will, but their nature is so pure and good—they are "the pure ones" (56:79)—that they do not disobey God (66:6).

Angels are the servants of God (43:19) who glorify and worship Him (13:13; 16:49), carry out His orders (16:50; 21:27), without in any way disobeying Him (66:6) or being remiss (6:61). They are not God's daughters (16:57; 37:150–152; 43:16, 19) who would intercede with Him on behalf of their votaries (53:26), guaranteeing them affluence in this world and salvation in the next (see *intercession*). They administer the universe according to the commandments of God (79:5). They serve as God's couriers (22:75; the literal meaning of *malak* is "messenger"), conveying messages from God to human beings—for example, to Zechariah (3:39) and Mary (3:42, 45)—and bringing down revelation from God to prophets (16:2). The Qur'ān was brought down by Gabriel, who is called the Holy Spirit (*q.v.*; 16:102). They keep watch on men (6:61; see also 13:11), recording their actions (10:21; 43:80; 50:17–18; 82:10–12). They are used by God to inflict punishment on rebellious nations (e.g. on the people of Lot: 51:32–34). They carry the Throne (*q.v.*) of God and surround it, glorifying God (40:7). They escorted the ark of the covenant (*q.v.*) back to the Israelites (2:248) and aided Muslims in the Battle of Badr (3:124–125; 8:9, 12). Two angels, Hārūt and Mārūt, were used by God to put the Jews in Babylon to a certain test

(2:102). In the hereafter, angels will serve as wardens of heaven (39:73) and hell (39:71; 40:49; 74:31). There are angels of death that draw out men's souls from their bodies at the appointed hour of death (4:97; 6:61, 93; 8:50; 16:32; 32:11).

Angels were commanded to bow before Adam (2:34; 7:11; 17:61; 18:50; 20:116). This implies that man is superior to them, though this superiority is potential and can be actualized only through the right kind of moral action on man's part (see *man*).

II. Significance of the Belief in Angels. Belief in angels is one of the articles of Islamic faith (see *faith*), and a brief explanation of why the Qur'ān considers the belief important (2:177, 285; 4:136) may not be out of place. Angels occupied a central position in Arabian mythology. They were thought to be the daughters of God, their principal function being to intercede with God for their votaries, making sure that the latter's prayers and wishes were granted by God—prayers for children and wealth in this world, wishes for salvation and good things in the next. This view of angels was based on the assumption that God did not have direct control of the world: being too far removed from the world of man, God could be reached only through intermediaries. Since the Qur'ān placed great emphasis on God's immediate concern with the affairs of man and on His involvement in history (see *Allāh*), it had to stress the need for the right belief in angels, who in the Arabian thought-world were such a hindrance to the right belief in God. Otherwise, belief in angels is like a footnote to the belief in God and may be subsumed under the latter, for it represents the negative aspect of the monotheistic creed: while belief in God means that there is only One God, belief in angels means that angels do not partake of the deity of God.

See also: HOLY SPIRIT, THE; INTERCESSION; JINN; SATAN.

ANIMAL VENERATION

The Qur'ān refers to the pagan Arabs' superstitious practice of venerating certain animals. The reference, in 5:103, is a brief one—four types of animals are named and the practice of venerating them criticized—and so brief details are in order.

1. *Baḥīrah.* Literally "a slit-eared she-camel," *baḥīrah* was the name given to a she-camel that had brought forth five young ones, the last one a male. Superstition regarded such a she-camel as worthy of honor. Accordingly, she was neither ridden nor milched, and, her ears slit, was allowed to roam about free and graze and drink anywhere she liked.

2. *Sā'ibah.* The *sā'ibah* was the she-camel which her owner had allowed to go free in fulfillment of his vow that, upon recovery from illness, he would neither ride nor milch her but would let her roam about free.

3. *Waṣīlah.* When a goat had brought forth two kids, one male and the other female, the male kid was not slaughtered but was allowed to go free in the name of gods. This male kid was called *waṣilah.*

4. *Ḥāmī.* A camel whose offspring's offspring had become strong enough to serve as a riding beast, or one which had sired ten young ones, was known as *ḥāmī.* Like the above-mentioned animals, the *ḥāmī* was left free to roam about and graze and drink unchecked.

ANṢĀB See LAWFUL AND THE UNLWFUL, THE

ANṢĀR See HELPERS, THE

APOSTASY

Arabic: *irtidād.*

Traditional Islamic law prescribes the penalty of death

for a Muslim who commits apostasy. The punishment is not stated in the Qur'ān, but is said to be based on certain *aḥādīth*. The advocates and the opponents of the said penalty have, in their attempt to find Qur'ānic support for their views, appealed to certain Qur'ānic verses, but the fact is that none of the arguments offered do full justice to the Qur'ānic context. All that the Qur'ān says on the subject is that the good actions of one who dies an apostate lose their worth in this world and in the next (2:217); that the repentance of one who first believes and then disbelieves, becoming more and more confirmed in his disbelief, will not be accepted (3:90); and that God will not forgive those who believe, then disbelieve, then believe, then diseblieve, becoming more and more entrenched in their disbelief (4:137).

See also: COMPULSION; DISSIMULATION.

APPOINTED TIME, THE

Arabic: *ajal; ajal musamman.*

Ajal, or *ajal musamman*, means "appointed time, fixed period of time." In some verses the two expressions are used in a non-technical sense, as in 2:282: "When you contract a loan for a fixed period of time (*ajal musamman*). . . ." (see also 22:33; 28:28). As a technical term, they refer to (a) the fixed life-span of an individual (6:128; 39:42; 40:67; 63:11), (b) the appointed time for the destruction of a wicked people (7:34; 10:49; 16:61; 20:129), or (c) the unalterable time appointed by God for the bringing about of the hereafter (*q.v.*; 46:3). In 6:2, the first *ajal* carries meaning (a) while the second *ajal*, which is qualified by *musamman*, represents meaning (c). The notion of *ajal* emphasizes, first, the finiteness of the period of time alloted to individuals and nations for moral action, and, second, the unalterability of that period of time, the moral of it all being that man must be constantly heedful of the reckoning of the Last Day (see *the hereafter*).

ARBITRATION

Arabic: *ḥukm.*

Arbitration may be used to settle disputes. Thus, in the case of a serious matrimonial discord, two arbitrators may be appointed, one from the man's family and one from the woman's, to reconcile the estranged spouses (4:35).

By recognizing and sanctioning arbitration as a parajudicial institution, the Qur'ān seeks to provide means for solving disputes on a more informal level. In the case of a matrimonial discord, the arbitrators' decision, the wording of 4:35 suggests, will be of the nature of a recommendation.

ARḌ AL-MUBĀRAKAH, AL- See BLESSED LAND, THE

ARḌ AL-MUQADDASAH, AL- See BLESSED LAND, THE

ARK OF THE COVENANT, THE

Arabic: *tābūt.*

The "ark of the covenant" (Num. 10:33; Deut. 31:26, etc.)—also known as the "ark of the testimony" (Exod. 25:16, 22) or the "ark of God" (I Sam. 3:3; 4:11)—was a chest containing certain sacred relics of the Israelites. The ark, which had great religious significance and served as a symbol of Israelite unity and pride, was lost to the Philistines in a battle about 1050 B.C. In the Qur'ān it is mentioned in connection with the election of Ṭālūt (Old Testament: Saul) as king of the Israelites. According to 2:246–248, the Israelites asked their prophet (Samuel) to appoint a king for them. When Samuel chose Ṭālūt as king, the Israelites objected that Ṭālūt, who possessed neither riches nor rank, was unfit to be their leader. Samuel told them that Ṭālūt's appointment carried divine sanction, to be manifested in the return of the ark. "The evidence of [the divine sanction of] his rule," Samuel says, referring to Ṭālūt, "is that the ark will come [back] to you, in it being solace from your Lord and remnants of things left behind by the family of Moses and the family of Aaron; angels will be carrying it" (2:248). Besides stating that the return of the ark would constitute a confirmation of Ṭālūt's election, the verse makes three points, which, following Iṣlāḥī, may be explained as follows:

First, the ark was a source of comfort for the Israelites. From the time of the Exodus to the time of the construction of the Temple in Jerusalem, the ark served as the focal point of Israelite religious life. It was considered sacred because it symbolized the presence of God, and its presence was taken to guarantee success in critical circumstances; as such, it was carried in the van of the army (e.g. Num. 10:33). This being the case, the loss of the ark was a national disaster, and its return, in the reign of Ṭālūt, would be an occasion for great rejoicing.

Second, the relics and mementos in the ark included certain objects pertaining to the families of Moses and Aaron. The return of the ark would thus signal the restoration, under Ṭālūt, of the glory of the times of Moses and Aaron.

Third, the ark was to be brought back by angels. According to I Samuel 6:7–14, the cart carrying the ark was pulled by two milch-cows, which, though undriven, went straight to Bethshemesh. An extraordinary event like this could have taken place only under the direction of angels.

ᶜARSH See THRONE

ASCENSION

I. Ascension of Jesus. According to the Qur'ān, Jesus did not die on the cross, but was rescued by God, Who raised him unto Himself (3:55; 4:158). Grammatically, the use of the preposition *ilā* ("to") after the verb *rafa*^{c}*a* ("to raise") in 4:158 and after the active participle *rāfi*^{c} in 3:55 establishes positively that the Qur'ān has in mind a physical lifting, and not simply a metaphorical lifting, i.e. the raising of Jesus' status.

II. Ascension of Muḥammad. 17:1 relates in these words what is generally called the "ascension" of Muḥammad: "Glorified is He Who took His servant [Muḥammad] by night from the Sacred Mosque [*q.v.*] to the Distant Mosque [*q.v.*], whose precincts We have blessed, in order that We might show him some of Our signs. . . ." The word *isrā'* in the verse literally means "to travel by night." While the Qur'ān mentions only the Prophet's journey from the Ka^{c}bah in Makkah to the Temple in Jerusalem, *Ḥadīth* describes in more detail the journey from the Temple to the heavens and the various kinds of experiences the Prophet had in the various phases of the journey.

According to 17:60, the ascension of Muḥammad was a *ru'yā*. While *ru'yā* may be translated "dream, vision," the Qur'ān seems to be implying (cf. 37:102–105) that a prophet's *ru'yā* is characterized by certitude, is free of doubt, and should not be confused with "imagination" or "fancy." *Ru'yā*, after all, is one of the channels through which a prophet receives revelation (*q.v.*) from God.

A more important question is: What is the significance of the journey from the Ka^{c}bah to the Temple in Jerusalem? According to one interpretation, the incident symbolizes the entrusting of Muslims, the new "elected community" (see *election*), with the task of providing to the world the religious and spiritual guidance of which the two houses of worship were the most important centers.

AṢḤĀB AL-MASH'AMAH See DEED-SCROLL

AṢḤĀB AL-MAYMANAH See DEED-SCROLL

AṢḤĀB AL-YAMĪN See DEED-SCROLL

AṢḤĀB ASH-SHIMĀL See DEED-SCROLL

ASMĀ' AL-ḤUSNĀ, AL- See ALLĀH

ATONEMENT

Arabic: *fidyah, kaffārah.*

I. Meaning. *Fidyah* means "ransom, redemption," and *kaffārah* "that which conceals." A good act atones for an act of commission or omission by "redeeming" or "concealing" it. True atonement, however, is not simply making formal amends for the wrong done, but is made, as 4:92 implies, with sincere feelings of repentance (*q.v.*). The standard forms of making atonement are fasting, giving charity, sacrificing an animal, and freeing a slave. Since slavery (*q.v.*) does not exist today, it has been suggested that the equivalent of the price of of a slave may be given in charity as a substitute.

II. Occasions and Forms. The Qur'ān speaks of the following occasions on which atonement is to be made:

1. *Sickness.* If, during the pilgrimage (*q.v.*), owing to an ailment, one has to shave one's head before offering animal sacrifice, one must either fast, give charity, or slaughter an animal (2:196).

2. *Failure to Make Sacrifice.* If a visiting pilgrim (that is, one who is not a resident of Makkah) decides to perform *ḥajj* and *ᶜumrah* (see *pilgrimage*), and, after performing the *ᶜumrah,* puts off *iḥrām* (see *pilgrimage*) with the intention of putting it on again for the *ḥajj,* he should offer an animal in sacrifice; if he cannot do so, he must fast three days during the pilgrimage and seven days after the completion of the piligrimage (2:196).

3. *Manslaughter.* 4:92 lays down the following rules for making amends for killing another Muslim by accident

(deliberate killing of another Muslim being unthinkable, and, according to 4:93, entailing eternal punishment in hell). If the person killed belongs to the Islamic State, the killer must free a Muslim slave and offer bloodwit (*q.v.*); if he belongs to a hostile non-Islamic State, only a slave will have to be freed; and if he belongs to a State with which the Islamic State has a pact, the killer shall pay bloodwit and also free a Muslim slave. If the killer does not possess the means to free a slave, he shall fast for a period of two months without break.

4. *Improper Oath.* A person who swears an oath to do something unlawful or improper must break it and, in atonement, feed or clothe ten poor people or free a slave; if he lacks the means to do so, he is required to fast three days (5:89). Atonement must also be made in the case of *ẓihār* (see *divorce*).

5. *Hunting.* If a person who is in a state of *iḥrām* kills an animal during *iḥrām*, he must atone for the act by offering an animal in sacrifice, to be sent to the Kaᶜbah, or feed a few people, or fast; what kind of animal shall be offered, what number of people fed, and how many days fasted shall be determined by two just and honest Muslims (5:95).

According to 5:45, if a person forgives a wrong done to him by someone and does not insist on taking revenge, his act of forgiveness will serve as atonement for his sins.

See also: DIVORCE; REPENTANCE.

AUTHORITY

4:59 explains the structure of authority in a Muslim community: "O those who have believed, obey God and obey the Prophet, and [obey] those in authority among you. Then, if you disagree in a matter, refer it back to God and the Prophet if you believe in God and the hereafter." The verse establishes several principles:

1. God and the Prophet must be obeyed in all matters.

2. In addition to God and the Prophet, "those in authority" must be obeyed.

3. "Those in authority" may be differed with, but God and the Prophet cannot be differed with but must command unquestioned obedience.

4. In case a difference of opinion occurs—whether between those in authority on the one hand and the common people on the other, or among those in authority themselves, the matter in question must be referred back to God and the Prophet.

A few points need to be noted. First, "God" in the verse stands for the Book of God. Similarly, "the Prophet" stands for the *Sunnah* of Muḥammad, for the verse addresses not only the Muslims of the Prophet's time but also those who would come after him, and it is the Prophet's *Sunnah* which can serve as a substitute for the Prophet after him. Second, the "referring of matters back to God and the Prophet" means that, where an issue cannot be solved in accordance with the letter of Qur'ān and *Sunnah*, it should be solved in accordance with the spirit of the two sources. Third, "those in authority" apparently refers to rulers and administrators, but it may equally refer to scholars and intellectuals—in fact to all those who are in a position to provide guidance and leadership to the Muslim community.

The Arabic for "those in authority" in 4:59 is *ulū l-amr*. The phrase also occurs in 4:83, where the *ulū l-amr* are described as those who have the ability to draw correct inferences. This implies that authority or leadership in Islam rightfully belongs to those who possess insight and learning, and that Islam does not recognize any form of hereditary, aristocratic, or oligarchic rule.

See also: CONSULTATION, PRINCIPLE OF.

ĀYAH

Āyah (pl. *āyāt*) has several meanings in the Qur'ān, all of which are interrelated through the literal meaning of "sign," some being at times interchangeable with others:

1. Hint, pointer, indication: 3:13 (the defeat of the Quraysh at the hands of Muslims in 624 was a signal to the effect that Islam would ultimately triumph over idolatry in Arabia), 41 (Zechariah's prayer for a sign that would assure him that a son would be born to him in his old age; also 19:10).

2. Evidence or proof, found in any part of the universe, including man's own being, that establishes, confirms, or vindicates certain truths or realities: 10:92; 19:21 (Jesus' miraculous birth as a proof of the hereafter, since the hereafter will be made possible, as was Jesus' birth, by the simple command of "Be!" given by God); 30:20–25, 46; 41:37, 39, 53; 42:29; 51:20–21.

3. Miracle (*q.v.*) performed by a prophet or demanded by a people: 2:118, 211; 6:25, 37, 109; 7:73; 17:101.

4. A verse of a revealed book: 2:106, 129, 151; 8:31; 10:15; 16:101; 65:11; 83:13.

AYYĀM ALLĀH See DAYS OF GOD, THE

AZLĀM See DIVINATION

B

BACKBITING

Arabic: **ghībah, ightiyāb.*

49:12 prohibits backbiting in these words: "Let there be no backbiting among you. Would any of you like to eat the flesh of his dead brother? The idea you would detest!"

"To eat someone's flesh" is an idiom in Arabic and means "to backbite someone." The image of eating someone's flesh implies that the victim of backbiting, being absent from the scene, is, like a corpse against a wild beast, defenseless against the malicious attacker. In other words, what makes backbiting a repulsive act is the cowardly attitude of the backbiter: feeling secure against a possible rejoinder from the victim, he indulges in the act. By using the words "dead brother" the Qur'ān makes the image much more forceful, and also provides typical Islamic grounds for the prohibition of a reprehensible practice: Muslims, according to 49:10 (and other verses), are "brothers" to one another (see *brotherhood*), and so it does not behoove them to indulge in backbiting.

BAGHY See DĪN

BAHĪMAT AL-ANᶜĀM See SACRIFICE

BAḤĪRAH See ANIMAL VENERATION

BALĀ' See TRIAL

BALANCE See MĪZĀN

BALDAH AL-MUḤARRAMAH, AL- See SACRED MOSQUE, THE

BAPTISM See HUE OF GOD, THE

BARZAKH

Barzakh literally means "barrier," and occurs in this sense in 25:53 and 55:20. As a technical term it denotes the period between death and resurrection—the period being a "barrier" between this life and the next. When a man dies, he enters into a state of *barzakh* "up until the day when people will be resurrected" (23:100).

According to the Qur'ān, the period of *barzakh* is not one of complete inactivity or dormancy; rather, during it a man gets a foretaste of his fate in the next life. 40:46 says that Pharaoh and his followers "are being exposed to fire day and night" during *barzakh* (the word does not occur in the verse, but the meaning is clear enough) and will receive greater punishment in the hereafter. Similarly, those who have died in the path of God "are being provided sustenance" (3:169). The Qur'ān would thus appear to attribute consciousness to man in *barzakh*. The precise nature of that consciousness cannot of course be determined. But it has been suggested that, depending on one's performance in this world, one experiences in *barzakh* pain or pleasure in the same way as in a dream. Like the pleasure and plain felt in a dream, the reward and punishment experienced during *barzakh* will be real enough for the experient, though the *barzakh* experience, unlike the dream experience, will not be entirely imaginary but will have an objectivity of its own.

From the Qur'ānic account it is obvious that *barzakh* cannot be likened to purgatory.

See also: DEATH; HEAVEN; HELL.

BASE DESIRES See HAWĀ

BASHĪR See GIVER OF GOOD TIDINGS

BATHING

Arabic: **ghusl, ightisāl.*

Bathing is required in order to remove major impurity (*q.v.*; 4:43). If one is unable to bathe because of lack of water or because one is sick or on a journey, one may make dry ablution (*q.v.*). A woman must bathe after her menstruation before one can have intercourse with her (2:222).

See also: ABLUTION; DRY ABLUTION; IMPURITY.

BĀṬIL See FALSEHOOD

BAYᶜAH See OATH OF ALLEGIANCE

BAYT AL-ᶜATĪQ, AL- See ANCIENT HOUSE, THE

BAYT AL-ḤARĀM, AL- See SACRED MOSQUE, THE

BAYT AL-MUḤARRAM, AL- See SACRED MOSQUE, THE

BAYYINAH See MANIFEST PROOF

BELIEF See FAITH

BEQUEST

Arabic: *waṣiyyah.*

Before the revelation of the law of inheritance (see *inheritance, law of*), every Muslim was supposed to make, at the time of his death, a bequest in favor of his parents and relatives (2:180). Also, 2:240 enjoined that those who are approaching death should leave instructions that their wives should be provided maintenance for one year and allowed to remain in the house during that period.

4:11–12, which contain the law of inheritance, supersede 2:180, 240, but do not exclude altogether the making of a bequest. According to 2:180, making a bequest is "obligatory," and, according to 4:11–12, the designated shares will be given only after the terms of the bequest have been fulfilled (and any outstanding debts paid). The implication is that the bequest can be made only in favor of other than the designated heirs. The amount one may bequeath is limited by *Ḥadīth* to one-third of the estate.

5:106 says that if death approaches one during a journey and one has to make a bequest, one should take two reliable Muslims as witnesses to the bequest; non-Muslims may be taken as witnesses if no Muslims are present.

See also: INHERITANCE, LAW OF.

BIDDING SELF, THE

Arabic: *an-nafs al-ammārah.*

"The bidding self" is that part of the human self (*nafs*) which tempts man to commit evil. The expression is used in 12:53, where Joseph, after successfully resisting the temptation from Potiphar's wife, says that, unless God were to protect one, one would succumb to the urgings of the *nafs* to commit evil.

See also: CENSORIOUS SELF, THE; CONTENTED SELF.

BIGHĀ' See COMPULSION

BIRR See PIETY

BLACK STREAK, THE See WHITE STREAK, THE

BLASPHEMY

Arabic: *ilḥād.*

Ilḥād has been used in the sense of "to blaspheme": "Leave those people alone who blaspheme His names" (7:180); "Those who blaspheme Our verses [or: signs] are not unknown to Us" (41:40). To blaspheme the name of God means: to predicate of God that which is unbecoming of His Being and does not agree with His attributes. To blaspheme the verses or signs of God means: to distort and misinterpret them and oppose them.

BLESSED LAND, THE

Arabic: *al-arḍ al-mubārakah.*

The region of Canaan-Palestine is called "the Blessed Land" (7:137; 21:71, 81; 34:18) because of the many blessings—material and spiritual—that were given to its inhabitants. In 5:21 it is called the Holy Land (*al-arḍ al-muqaddasah*), doubtless because of the preaching in it of the—holy—monotheistic creed by Abraham and his successors.

BLESSING

Arabic: *barakah* (pl. *barakāt*).

Barakah denotes material good or spiritual gift, or, as in 7:96, both. In the Qur'ān the following are called blessed:

1. Human beings: Noah (11:48), Abraham and Isaac (37:113), Abraham's wife Sarah (11:73), and Jesus (19:31).

2. Places: the Ka^{c}bah (3:96), the Temple of Jerusalem (17:1), the spot in the Sinai where God spoke to Moses (28:30), Canaan-Palestine (see *the blessed land*), and the earth as a whole (41:10).

3. Natural phenomena: the Night of Decree (*q.v.*; 44:3), the olive tree (24:35), bounteous rain (50:9).

4. The Qur'ān: 6:92, 155; 21:50; 38:29.

5. Acts, events: greeting (24:61), safe arrival (23:29).

The source of all blessings is God, Who is therefore called Blessed (7:54; 23:14; 25:1, 10, 61; 27:8; 40:64; 43:85; 55:78; 67:1).

BLOOD See LAWFUL AND THE UNLAWFUL, THE

BLOODWIT

Arabic: *diyah*.

The survivors or relatives of a person killed can demand that the killer be put to death (see *qiṣāṣ*); alternatively, they may choose to accept bloodwit (2:178).

The Qur'ānic notion of bloodwit differs from the pre-Islamic Arabian notion. In Islam, bloodwit is *one* of the options open to the wronged party and not, as was sometimes the case in pre-Islamic times, the *only* option open to it. A powerful tribe might not allow its member, a killer, to be put to death by a weak tribe whose member had been killed and insist on paying bloodwit. In the Qur'ān, the decision to accept or reject bloodwit rests with the aggrieved party. But since voluntary acceptance of bloodwit is indicative of leniency toward the aggressor party and holds out a hope for an eventual reconciliation between the two parties, 2:178 subtly suggests that bloodwit be accepted ("So, if one is shown a measure of lenience by his brother . . ."), advising the aggressor party, if its offer of bloodwit is accepted, to pay the amount honestly and with a sense of gratitude.

See also: ATONEMENT; QIṢĀṢ.

BOOK See KITĀB

BREACH OF TRUST

Arabic: *khiyānah; ikhtiyān.*

8:27 forbids one to commit a breach of trust. The word "trust" in the verse is to be taken in an extended sense (see *trust*).

Being untrue to oneself is to commit *khiyānah.* To have intercourse with one's wife at night in the month of Ramaḍān (*q.v.*) was not unlawful, but some Muslims thought it was. So, when they had intercourse with their wives during Ramaḍān nights, they acted against their own conscience, and 2:187 calls it a breach of trust.

In 4:107, the Hypocrites (*q.v.*) are accused of committing a breach of trust against themselves. The word *ikhtiyān* in this verse has overtones of "wifely infidelity": like an unfaithful wife who plays false to her husband, the Hypocrites claim to be faithful to God and the Prophet but in fact support the cause of unbelief.

In the political sphere, if Muslims have a pact with a non-Muslim people and there are clear indications that the latter intends to break the pact, this fear of *khiyānah* gives Muslims the right to terminate the pact, though they must duly inform the other party of their decision to do so (8:71).

The word *khiyānah,* used in 66:10 with reference to the wives of Noah and Lot, does not mean wifely infidelity, but refers to the two women's failure to support their husbands in the latter's struggle against evil and their betrayal of their husbands at crucial moments.

See also: TRUST.

BROTHERHOOD

Arabic: **ukhuwwah.*

Muslims are called brothers to one another—"brothers

in religion" (33:5). The bond of Islam which provided a strong basis for unifying the divided tribes of Arabia, is described as a special favor of God to Muslims (3:103).

I. Rights and Duties. The brotherhood of Islam establishes certain rights and duties. If two factions of Muslims fight each other, other Muslims may not sit on the fence, but must take appropriate measures to bring the fighting to an end (49:9–10; see *civil war*). 49:12 makes the brotherhood of Muslims the basis for the prohibition of backbiting (*q.v.*).

As a rule, the religious bond of brotherhood does not create legal rights and obligations. It does not, for example, create rights of inheritance (see *inheritance, law of*) or raise impediments to marriage (*q.v.*). Nevertheless, it is sometimes invoked to facilitate the smooth functioning of the legal apparatus or to remove complications that might arise in certain situations. Thus 2:178 subtly invokes Islamic brotherhood as grounds for accepting bloodwit instead of demanding execution of the killer (see *bloodwit*), and in 2:220 guardians are permitted to manage the property of the orphans under their care by "intermixing" their property with their own because "they are your brothers." We have already noted that, in the event of a war between two Muslim groups, other Muslims cannot remain neutral.

II. Prophet as Brother to His People. A prophet is often called in the Qur'ān a "brother" to his people (7:65, 73, 85; 11:50, 61, 84; 26:106, 124, 142, 161; 27:45; 29:36; 46:21), and that in two senses. First, having lived in the midst of his people for a long time before announcing his prophecy, he is as well known to them as is one's brother to one, his unblemished character, to which they are first-hand witnesses, establishing a moral claim upon them to listen to his message and accept it. Second, a prophet is a well-wisher of his people, just as one brother is a well-wisher of another.

See also: WALĀYAH.

BUKHL See MISERLINESS

BURHĀN See MANIFEST PROOF

BURNT OFFERING See SACRIFICE

C

CALIPH

Arabic: *khalīfah* (pl. *khulafā', khalā'if*).

I. Ethical Concept. In 2:30 man is called "caliph." Since "caliph" means "successor, vicegerent," the question arises, Who is man a successor to? Did he succeed another order of creation—the *jinn* (*q.v.*), as has been suggested—or was he appointed the vicegerent of God? There is hardly any support for the first view, certainly none in the Qur'ān, whereas the second view does have Qur'ānic support, as in the verses which state that God has created all things for man, giving him control over everything (22:65; 31:20; 45:13), and that man has been charged with a responsibility the heavens and the earth excused themselves from bearing (33:72; see *trust*).

Why was man made the caliph of God? The Adam story in S. 2 (vss. 30–39) implies, and also indicates more clearly (vss. 38–39), that the purpose of man's creation was to see whether, using the freedom of choice he has been given, he accepts or rejects the divine guidance that he would receive. In the broader Qur'ānic context, man was created in order to be put to the test—"in order that He may try you and find out which of you perform good actions" (67:2; see *trial*). As God's vicegerent, then, man's position is one of privilege and responsibility both: on the one hand he enjoys the freedom of choice and action, on the other he is supposed to make responsible use of that freedom. The vicegerency of which 2:30 speaks is thus essentially moral in character.

II. Political Concept. Elsewhere the word "caliph" is used to denote a political ruler, as in 7:69, 74, and 38:26, though the moral notion of vicegerency is not excluded, as can be seen from 10:14, which describes moral trial as the purpose of investing a people with caliphate.

See also: MAN; TRIAL.

CENSORIOUS SELF, THE

Arabic: *an-nafs al-lawwāmah.*

The censorious self (75:2) is that part of the human self (*nafs*) which, representing the element of goodness in his nature, censures him before or after committing an evil act. In other words, it is the conscience of man. It is opposed to "the bidding self" (*q.v.*).

See also: BIDDING SELF, THE; CONTENTED SELF, THE.

CHANCE COMPANION

Arabic: *aṣ-ṣāḥib bi l-janb.*

4:36 enjoins that one should treat one's "chance companion" kindly. A chance companion (the Arabic expression literally means "companion by one's side") is any person in whose company one happens to find oneself in a certain situation or on a given occasion, for example during a journey.

CHARITY See ṢADAQAH; ZAKĀT

CHASTITY

Arabic: *iḥṣān.*

Chastity, or sexual purity, is a virtue the Qur'ān extols and upholds. Mary, mother of Jesus, is praised for her chastity (21:91; 66:12), and Muslims are expected to live chaste lives, sex being allowed only between marriage partners or between a man and his female slave (see *slavery*). Marriage (*q.v.*) is regarded as guaranteeing chastity, and penalties are imposed for adultery (*q.v.*) and false allegation of unchastity (*q.v.*). Besides establishing the institution of marriage on firm grounds, the Qur'ān gives general instructions to safeguard chastity. Both men (24:30) and women (24:31) are asked to "keep their eyes lowered," and women are instructed to cover themselves properly (24:31), especially upon leaving home (33:59), and not to speak with strangers in an inviting tone (33:32).

See also: ADULTERY; DRESS; FALSE ALLEGATION OF UNCHASTITY; IMMORALITY; MARRIAGE; SLAVERY.

CHORD OF GOD, THE

Arabic: *ḥabl Allāh.*

I. Basis of Unity. Muslims are instructed to hold fast to the "chord of God" and not to split into factions (3:103). The "chord of God" stands for the religion of Islam, which furnishes the principal basis of Muslim unity. Islam has been so called because on the one hand it establishes a relationship between God and the believers, and on the other hand unites all believers into a brotherhood (*q.v.*). The instruction to Muslims to hold fast to the chord of God means that they should focus on the fundamental teachings of that religion and avoid attaching too much importance to peripheral and minor issues, which can easily lead to division and dissension.

II. Chord as Covenant. The expression "chord of God," as used in 3:103, also contains the notion of covenant (*q.v.*), since the Arabic for "chord," *ḥabl*, frequently denotes "agreement, pact." Thus "to join one's chord to another's" means "to make an agreement with someone," and "to break the chord" is "to sever one's relations with somebody." Since the injunction, in 3:103, to avoid schism is prefaced with the injunction to hold fast to the chord of God, the implication is that Muslims can avoid schisms and achieve true unity only by fulfilling the terms of their covenant with God.

III. Chord as Protection. In 3:112 the "chord of God" means "protection given in the name of God," i.e. protection given by an Islamic power through a pact, the "chord of people" (*ḥabl an-nās*) in the same verse referring to protection given by a non-Islamic power.

See also: FIRM HANDLE, THE.

CHORD OF PEOPLE, THE See CHORD OF GOD, THE

CIRCUMAMBULATION See PILGRIMAGE

CIVIL WAR

49:9 reads: "If two factions of believers engage in fighting, reconcile them. Then if one of them commits aggression against the other, fight the one that is the aggressor until it should come back to the commandment of God. If it does, then reconcile the two in accordance with justice. Act justly; God loves the just."

This verse lays down a number of rules for resolving an armed conflict between Muslims. First, if two parties of Muslims should fight with each other, the rest of the Muslim community cannot sit in the neutral corner, but must intervene in order to end the conflict. Second, the intervention is not limited to making appeals and passing resolutions, but includes possible military action. Third, this military action shall be taken after negotiations have failed and against the party that is found to be the aggressor. Fourth, in bringing about a reconciliation between two warring factions of Muslims, the other Muslims must not show prejudice for or against one of the faction but must act in strict accordance with justice.

See also: FIGHTING AGAINST GOD AND HIS PROPHET; JIHĀD.

COMPANION, CHANCE See CHANCE COMPANION

COMPETITION

Arabic: *takāthur; musābaqah.*

Competition for greater worldly glory is called *takāthur* in the Qur'ān and is condemned: "Race for more utterly engrossed you, until you paid the visit to graves" (102:2). For the Arabs, "race for more" or *takāthur* was the desire for greater wealth and (since a larger family meant more power within the clan and without) more children (57:20). Instead of competing for worldly goods, one should, the Qur'ān advises, compete in the field of good actions (2:148), aiming to win God's forgiveness and paradise (57:21; 83:26).

COMPULSION

Arabic: *ikrāh.*

Misdeeds committed by a person under compulsion will not be held against him by God. In Arabia, owners of female slaves often forced them to engage in prostitution (*bighā'*) with a view to making money. 24:33 strictly forbids them to do so, saying that God will forgive the slaves who were compelled to engage in the practice.

Declaration of unbelief made by a Muslim under

duress will be forgiven by God (see *dissimulation*).

According to 2:256, there is no compulsion in religion (see *dīn*).

See also: DĪN; DISSIMULATION; NECESSITY.

CONDESCENSION

Arabic: *mann*.

The Qur'ān prohibits one who gives *ṣadaqah (q.v.)* to follow it up with *mann* (2:264), a word for which no adequate English translation exists but which may roughly be translated "condescension." *Mann* is to remind someone directly or indirectly of the favor one has done him and, by thus making him conscious of the debt that is owed, humiliate him. Such an act, according to the Qur'ān, nullifies the good deed of *ṣadaqah* (see *nullification of deeds*), depriving one of the reward of *ṣadaqah* (2:264).

See also: ṢADAQAH.

CONFEDERATES, THE

Arabic: *aḥzāb*.

The Qur'ān uses the term "confederates" principally to refer to the Arabian opponents of Islam. It sometimes refers to one member of the opposition, as in 11:17 (in which the Quraysh are referred to, although there is also a subtle reference to the People of the Book [*q.v.*], who had in the late Makkan period become secretly active in their opposition to Islam), sometimes to the Idolators (see *idolatry*) or the People of the Book (13:36), and sometimes to subgroups of the major groups of the opposition, as in 38:11 (clans of Quraysh) or 19:37 and 43:65 (subsects of Christianity).

The usage in 38:13 (40:5, 30 are similar) is to be noted. The verse refers to the peoples of Noah, ᶜĀd, Pharaoh, Thamūd, Lot, and Shuᶜayb. These peoples existed at different times, and so were not "confederates" in the sense that they put up a united front against any one prophet. However, each one of them is called *aḥzāb* because, in its opposition to its own prophet, it rallied together the divergent elements of society.

And here we may have a clue to the significance of the term *aḥzāb* as used in the Qur'ān. Being a plural of *ḥizb* ("party, faction"), the word implies that the opponents of Islam have a negative basis of unity: animosity toward Islam, and not commitment to positive goals held in common, is what brings them together, and at bottom they remain what they are—so many parties or *aḥzāb*.

CONFIDENTIAL TALK See NAJWĀ

CONSULTATION, PRINCIPLE OF

Arabic: *shūrā*.

According to 42:38, one of the distinctive features of Islamic society is the way in which matters of social importance are decided in it: "And their affairs are [run in accordance with the principle of] consultation among them." Modern Muslim scholars view the principle of consultation as the cornerstone of the Islamic political system and as the mark and measure of Islamic politics. In their attempt to work it out in detail, they have derived from the principle a set of norms and rules, positive and negative, some of which are: accountability of the executive; decentralization of power; elective government; and rejection of any form of government that repudiates the principle of consultation.

See also: AUTHORITY.

CONTENTED SELF, THE

Arabic: *an-nafs al-muṭma'innah*.

The contented self (89:27) is that which in all kinds of circumstances remains unshaken in its devotion to God.

The Arabic word *iṭmi'nān*, usually translated "contentment," denotes "stability, steadfastness": it is used of a rock that, after being in motion, comes to a rest and remains in that state. The contented self, then, is one that remains "unmoved" by fluctuations of fortune: circumstances of ease do not make it proud or smug, and times of hardship do not make it impatient or fretful. The reward for the contented self is paradise (89:30).

See also: BIDDING SELF, THE; CENSORIOUS SELF, THE.

CORRUPTION

Arabic: *fasād*.

The Arabic word has a wide range of meanings—"disorder, corruption, mischief, wrong, anarchy"—and stands for a breach of law, whether natural, moral, or social. Accordingly, *fasād* can take many forms. Had there been more than one deity, there would have been *fasād* or chaos in the universe (21:22). Pharaoh's oppressive measure of killing male Israelite children was an instance of *fasād* (28:4), as was the opposition of the nine clans to the prophet Ṣāliḥ (27:48).

The corruption that man causes in the world (30:41) is the result of misuse by him of the power to act freely (see *freedom and determininsm*). Man's power to act freely is, however, not unlimited, and God continually purges the *fasād* caused by man (2:251). It was because of the corruption they caused that many of the earlier nations were destroyed by God (7:86, 103; 27:14).

COVENANT

Arabic: *ᶜahd, mīthāq*.

The relationship between God and man is conceived in terms of a covenant. A covenant establishes certain rights and obligations. The covenant of God—the most important meaning of the terms *ᶜahd* and *mīthāq* in the Qur'ān—binds man to the worship of God to the exclusion of any other being, and, in return, gives man the promise of material and spiritual success, terrestrial and eschatological salvation. Whether the covenant is fulfilled or not depends on man: "Fulfill My covenant [i.e. your obligation toward Me] and I shall fulfill yours [i.e. My obligation toward you]" (2:40). The initiative, that is to say, has to come from man, for it is he whose fate is at stake.

The covenant between God and man takes several forms.

1. *Instinctual.* According to 7:172, God in preexistence extracted from the loins of men all humanity and bound it to His worship. "Am I not your Lord?" God asked, and all responded by saying, "Yes, indeed." This verse symbolically presents the urge to worship God as being innate to man. Man possesses an instinctual awareness of his bond with God, though this awareness and inclination may be sharpened or deadened by circumstances and by the moral choices one makes.

2. *Prophetical.* The prophetical covenant is that which is made through the agency of prophets. It takes the form of clear and definite pronouncements, in oral or written form, that a prophet conveys from God to his people. The Bible and the Qur'ān are instances of scriptural covenant, whereas earlier prophets, like Adam and Noah, received from God and brought to their peoples oral communications.

The instinctual and prophetical covenants differ from each other in a few respects. The former is immediate in that it is made directly with every human being, whereas the latter is mediate in that it is made through prophets. Furthermore, the former is logically and historically prior to the latter. Finally, the former establishes accountability in a general way, whereas the latter establishes it in a more specific and comprehensive manner.

These differences notwithstanding, the two types of covenants complement each other. For, in the people who have preserved the goodness of their nature (see *fiṭrah*), the instinctual awareness of God is aroused to full activity by the prophetical covenant, the combination of the two accounting for the enthusiastic response of such people to the call of prophets. The inner light of nature possessed by such people is reinforced by the outer light of the prophetic message, so that they come to possess, in the words of 24:35, "light upon light."

3. *Occasional.* There is a third kind of covenant, one that is made between God and man on a given occasion with respect to a given matter. This covenant itself may take more than one form: the covenant made by God with a certain individual, as with Abraham (2:124–125), and the covenant that an individual makes either with God or with another person in the name of God (16:91).

All three types of covenants—instinctual, prophetical, and occasional—are to be fulfilled, and the commandment to fulfill the covenant of God (2:40; 6:152) applies to all types, some verses (like 17:34) enjoining the fulfillment of "covenant" in absolute terms.

See also: FIṬRAH; GUIDANCE; REMEMBRANCE; TRUST.

CRITERION, THE

Arabic: *furqān.*

Furqān is "that which sets one thing apart from another," and is usually translated "criterion, distinction." The Torah and the Qur'ān are each called *furqān* (the former in 2:53 [taking the *wāw* between *tawrāt* and *furqān* as exegetical] and 21:48, the latter in 3:4 and 25:1) because the purpose of the revelation of the two books was to sift truth from falsehood. The day of the Battle of Badr is called "the day of distinction" (*yawm al-furqān*) in 8:41 because on that day a clear distinction was made between the upholders of truth and the supporters of falsehood. In 8:29 *furqān* stands for the "decisive victory" that will belong to truth when it appears in a manifest, unbeclouded form.

CURSE

Arabic: *la*^{c}*nah.*

I. Meaning. To be under the curse of God is to be deprived of God's blessings and be subject to His wrath.

II. Causes of the Infliction of a Curse. The curse of God is brought upon an individual or a people by a multiplicity of causes, in each case the person or people cursed being responsible for the curse. Among the causes are: defiance of God (4:117–118; 5:60); violation of the commandments of God (4:47; 13:25; 38:72–78; 5:78); breaking of the covenant of God (see *covenant*; 5:13; 13:25); disbelief in God and His message (2:89; 33:64); death in a state of disbelief (2:161); misrepresentation of His message (2:159); opposition to Him and His prophets (33:57); bringing of false allegation of unchastity against chaste persons (24:23); iniquity (*q.v.*; 7:44; 11:18; 40:52); gross lying (3:61); corruption (*q.v.*) in the earth (13:25; 47:23); hypocrisy (see *the hypocrites*; 33:61). The evildoers, once in hell, will curse one another (7:38; 29:25).

III. Result of the Curse. Once God puts a curse on a person, that person becomes incapable of receiving guidance (2:88; 4:46); it is as if one's heart has become hardened (5:13) and one has lost the power to see, hear, think, and judge (47:22–23; see *sealing*).

See also: ACCURSED TREE, THE; DOUBLE SWEARING; SEALING.

CUSTOMARY LAW

Arabic: *ma^{c}rūf.*

Ma^{c}rūf literally means "that which is familiar, recognized, well-known, reasonable." As a Qur'ānic term, it is used in a wide sense (see *enjoining good and forbidding evil*) and in a restricted sense. In its latter sense, the subject of the present article, *ma^{c}rūf* stands for that part of the customary law of pre-Islamic Arabia which the Qur'ān approves of and assimilates into Islam. Thus 4:25 suggests that the amount of dower (*q.v.*) a husband has to pay may be determined by the *ma^{c}rūf* of a given area, society, or class. According to 2:233, if a man has divorced his wife but would like her to nurse his infants, he should provide food and clothing to her in accordance with *ma^{c}rūf.* Similarly, if a man pronounces divorce (*q.v.*) once or twice, he should, at the end of the waiting period (*q.v.*), either take back his wife, in accordance with *ma^{c}rūf,* or effect a final separation, again in accordance with *ma^{c}rūf*; that is, he should, like a reasonable and honorable man, decide the matter one way or the other. *Ma^{c}rūf* thus serves as an important means of augmenting the corpus of Islamic law.

The Qur'ān used *ma^{c}rūf* to facilitate transition from pre-Islamic to Islamic law. For instance, before laying down the law of inheritance (see *inheritance, law of*) in its final form in 4:11–12, 176, the Qur'ān gave, in 2:180 a provisional statement of the law, and this provisional statement, as the verse indicates, accorded with pre-Islamic Arabian customary law.

See also: ENJOINING GOOD AND FORBIDDING EVIL.

D

ḌALĀL See MISGUIDANCE

ḌALĀLAH See MISGUIDANCE

DĀR AS-SALĀM See ABODE OF PEACE, THE

DAY OF JUDGMENT, THE See HEREAFTER, THE

DAYS OF GOD, THE

Arabic: *ayyām Allāh.*

The "days of God" are those historic events of the past which furnish unmistakable evidence of the meting out, by God, of recompense to nations. The expression occurs twice. In 14:5 Moses is asked to remind his people of the "days of God," that is, of instances in past history in which the steadfast in faith and virtue were blessed by God and the evil peoples punished. In 45:14 the believers are asked to avoid and ignore those who do not expect to see the "days of God," that is, do not think that God will punish the wicked.

DEATH

Arabic: *mawt.*

According to the Qur'ān, death is neither a mystery

nor "a sleep and a forgetting," but a stage of transition from one life to another, a stage that forms an integral part of the scheme of existence. During his earthly life man acts out his role as a moral agent and either succeeds or fails in that task; in the next life he will be recompensed for his actions. Death is thus a line of demarcation between life on earth and life in the hereafter: it closes the chapter of actions and opens that of recompense. Being only a stage of transition in the continuum of life-death-life, death does not mean complete extinction, but only separation of soul from body, and only a temporary separation at that.

One's death is "appointed" in the sense that the time (3:145) and place (31:34) of one's death have been unalterably fixed by God. It is thus futile to flee the battlefield in the hope of averting death (3:144–145, 156; 33:16; also 3:154, 168; 4:78).

Contrary to the notion of "you live only once," a notion the Qur'ān criticizes (23:37; 45:24; 50:3), the Qur'ān presents the notion of "you die only once" (see 44:56). For there *is* life after death, and that life will know no death. This will be one of the great joys of the people of paradise (44:57), but it will be one of the great sorrows of the people of hell, who will wish for death (14:17; 35:36).

In certain verses (as in 2:28; see also 40:11), the time before one's coming into existence is called the period of death. In 6:122 and 35:22, lack of awareness of certain realities is called death: one who lacks the light of true guidance is no better than one who is dead.

See also: BARZAKH; EARTHLY LIFE.

DEED-SCROLL

Arabic: *kitāb*.

Upon being resurrected in the next life, every human being will receive a "book" or "deed-scroll" containing a complete account of the way in which he lived his life (17:13,

14). Those who are to go to heaven shall hold their deed-scrolls in their right hands (17:71; 69:19–24; 84:7–9). They are the *aṣḥāb al-yamīn* ("people of the right hand" [56:27, 38; 74:39]); in 56:8 and 90:18 they are called *aṣḥāb al-maymanah*, an expression that has the same meaning as *aṣḥāb al-yamīn* but also means "the blessed people." Those who are to go to hell shall hold their deed-scrolls in their left hands (69:25–32); 84:10 adds that they will be handed their deed-scrolls from behind, which suggests that their hands will be tied behind their backs. These people are the *aṣḥāb ash-shimāl* ("people of the left hand" [56:41]); in 56:9 and 90:19 they are called *aṣḥāb al-mash'amah* ("the unfortunate people"). While the "people of the right hand" will rejoice and invite all to read their deed-scrolls (69:19), the "people of the left hand" will wish they had never received theirs (69:25).

See also: KITĀB.

DHIKR See REMEMBRANCE

DHIKRĀ See REMEMBRANCE

DĪN

I. Four Meanings. The word *dīn* has four meanings in the Qur'ān:

1. Submission, as in 16:52: "To Him belongs what is in the heavens and the earth, and it is to Him that submission must always be made" (see also 39:2).

2. A system of beliefs, or, roughly, religion, as in 3:83: "Do they desire a religion other than the religion of God?"

3. Law, as in 12:76: "It was not for him [Joseph] to detain his brother in accordance with the law of the king."

4. Recompense, as in 51:6: "And recompense shall be meted out."

The four meanings are interconnected, and we can see the connection if we take "submission" (1) as the essential meaning. A set of beliefs or tenets (2) is submission on the creedal level, whereas "law" (3) suggests law-abidingness, the submission now being on the plane of conduct. As for "recompense" (4), it represents the results of one's submission to God or defiance of Him.

II. Dīn as Law. A word may be said about the third of the four meanings. Use of the word *dīn* for "law" (the context in 12:76 gives the sense of "law of the land") explains why Islam is regarded as being a religion that is not only the private affair of its adherents but also deals with the public aspects of their life, that is, with the political, economic, and social aspects. The Qur'ān insists that the *dīn* must be practiced and implemented in its entirety (8:39), and that only God's *dīn* must be in force (9:33; 48:28; 61:9). The notion that Islam covers the "secular" or "profane" as well as the so-called religious and spiritual fields of life, that it is a complete way of life, thus has its basis in the Qur'ān itself.

The Qur'ānic use of the word *dīn* is one of many examples illustrating how the Qur'ān, taking words that were familiar to the Arabs, imbues them with new meanings. A common meaning of the word *dīn* in Arabic was "custom, practice," but the Qur'ān, so to speak, gave the word the upgraded meaning of "law." The meaning of "recompense," likewise, is construed by the Qur'ān in a much vaster sense than it was in the Arabic language before, the ethical notions of justice being largely absent from the pre-Islamic usage.

III. Rationale of Dīn. According to the Qur'ān, *dīn* is not an imposition on man but a necessary aid to him. Spread all around man, and geared to serve him, is a vast network of providential care. This phenomenon fills man with gratitude for an unseen bountiful being. Thus moved, man feels impelled to serve that being in humble gratitude, but does not know how to serve him. *Dīn* steps in and tells him how to do so. By clarifying a profound, albeit initially somewhat vague, human urge to worship God and providing proper channels for the expression of that urge, *dīn* supplies a deeply felt need of the human soul.

IV. History of Religion. The Qur'ān emphasizes (3:19) that there has been only one *dīn* revealed by God for mankind: "Islam" (*q.v.*). Since "Islam" means "submission," the statement in 3:19 implies that all prophets have taught the same essential message of submission to God (42:13), even though in point of detail religions may have differed considerably from one another. Abraham, a monotheist, is presented as the prototypical "Muslim" (see *Islam*), for with complete loyalty he submitted to the One God (see *ḥanīf*). Monotheism is thus the cornerstone of the perennial *dīn*, and was (as can be inferred from 3:33) the creed of the first man, Adam (cf. Gen. 4:26). If monotheism was mankind's original religion, then the different forms of idolatory constitute so many instances of falling away from that original religion. In other words, man has not "progressed" from polytheism to monotheism, but has degenerated from monotheism to polytheism. Discovery of monotheism is properly called *re*discovery of monotheism.

What led men away from the original *dīn*? Not ignorance of truth but willful rejection of it was the main cause. Self-righteousness has often prevented men from granting that truth could be found with others. The desire to monopolize truth has often led men to commit *baghy* ("injustice, wrong, oppression") against one another, and truth has suffered in the process (2:90, 213; 42:14; 45:17). Another major cause of the neglect or rejection of the original religion was parochialism (3:105). The fundamentals of religion were ignored and interest was focused on relatively minor issues in *dīn*.

It was said above that God has revealed the same essential *dīn* in the all ages. This does not, however, mean that *dīn* has never undergone any changes. The outer forms of *dīn* have changed from time to time, the changes having been determined by the needs and circumstances of different periods of human history. In any given period, that is to say, religion has possessed certain universal-permanent and certain local-temporal elements. Muḥammad is regarded as the final prophet (see *prophet; the seal of the prophets*), and the dispensation given by him, Islam, as the final religion. In Islam, in other words, *dīn* reaches its culmination or perfection (5:3).

V. No Compulsion in Religion. 2:256 says that there is no compulsion in religion. The meaning is that God has not compelled man to accept the truth, but has left him free to make his choice with regard to it, and that the responsibility for accepting the truth rests with the individual.

See also: ABROGATION; COVENANT; FIṬRAH; ISLAM; REMEMBRANCE.

DISBELIEF

Arabic: *kufr*.

The principal meaning of *kufr* in the Qur'ān is "to disbelieve," that is, to disbelieve in or reject God, a prophet, a scripture, the hereafter, the truth, etc. (2:126, 253, 258; 5:12; 16:106; 19:77; 30:44; 41:52; 60:1; 67:7; 90:19). *Kufr* is a major sin (see *major sin and minor sin*), one for which many nations in the past were destroyed (11:60, 68; 13:32; 34:15–19; 43:24–25; 47:10), and one which will receive grave punishment in the hereafter (*q.v.*; 2:7, 39, 126; 3:4, 12, 56; 4:56; 5:10; 9:3; 10:4; 18:106; 22:19; 57:19). Any good deeds performed in a state of disbelief will be nullified (14:18; 24:39; see *nullification of deeds*).

The root meaning of *kufr* is "to hide, conceal," and it underlies the meaning of "disbelief": to disbelieve is to hide the truth or deny recognition to it. The other meanings of *kufr* in the Qur'ān, again closely related to that of "disbelief," are as follows: (a) to disavow, disown (30:13; 35:14; 46:6); (b) to deprive, deny (3:115); and (c) to be ungrateful (16:55; 17:27; 29:66; 30:34 43:15).

See also: FAITH; GRATITUDE.

DISCIPLE

Arabic: *ḥawārī.*

The Qur'ān uses the word *hawārī* (pl. *ḥawāriyyūn*) for a disciple of Jesus. The literal meaning of *hawārī* is "sincere, devoted friend or supporter." In 3:52 Jesus asks his disciples, "Who will be my supporter [in the way leading] to God?" and they volunteered themselves enthusiastically. In 61:14 the Qur'ān cites the *ḥawāriyyūn* as model believers. The Qur'ān's praise of the *ḥawāriyyūn* suggests that, in the view of the Qur'ān, they did not abandon Jesus in his hour of need but stuck with him. 5:111 says that God "intimated" to the *ḥawāriyyūn* that they should believe in Him and in His prophet, Jesus, and that the *ḥawāriyyūn* did so.

5:112 reports the *ḥawāriyyūn* as asking Jesus whether God would send down a feast from the heaven—a request, presumably, for a miracle. The Qur'ān does not say whether the request was accepted, but Jesus' admonition, "Fear God if you are [true] believers," suggests that the *ḥawāriyyūn* did not insist that the miracle be shown. But the request is significant in that it indicates that the *ḥawāriyyūn* regarded God, and not Jesus, as the one who caused miracles to happen, Jesus in their view being only an agency through whom miracles were wrought.

See also: HELPERS, THE; MIRACLE.

DISCRIMINATION BETWEEN PROPHETS

Arabic: *tafrīq bayn ar-rusul.*

To "discriminate between prophets" (2:136, 285; 3:84;

4:150) is to believe in some prophets but not in others. Such a discrimination is, according to the Qur'ān, unwarranted because all prophets have preached the same truths, and only arrogance, prejudice, or partisanship can prevent one from accepting the truth in its many manifestations. The prophets, as Shāh Walī Allāh says, are like consanguine brothers.

See also: PROPHECY.

DISSIMULATION

Arabic: **taqiyyah*.

According to 16:106, fear of persecution is a legitimate excuse for hiding one's faith; one may even verbally renounce one's faith, provided one remains unshaken in one's heart. The verse, however, warns against abusing the permission by "opening up one's breast to disbelief," that is, by actually becoming an unbeliever.

While conditions of fear may permit one to conceal one's faith, there are situations in which it is more laudable to declare one's faith than to conceal it, even if profession of faith means putting one's life in jeopardy. 40:28–45 tell the story of "one of the people of Pharaoh" who believed in Moses but had concealed his faith. When Pharaoh threatened to kill Moses, the "believing man" boldly declared which side he was on and gave open support to Moses.

Contrary to the generally held view, 3:28, the supposed source of the term *taqiyyah*, has nothing to do with the subject, the view being based on a misreading of the clause of exception in the verse.

See also: COMPULSION.

DISTANT MOSQUE, THE

Arabic: *al-masjid al-aqṣā*.

The Temple at Jerusalem is so called (17:1; the Arabic

literally means "the farther mosque") because it is at a considerable distance from Makkah.

See also: ASCENSION; SACRED MOSQUE, THE.

DISTORTION OF SCRIPTURE

Arabic: *ikhfā'*; *layy*; *taḥrīf.*

The People of the Book (*q.v.*) are accused of distorting the scriptures—according to Muslim scholars, particularly those portions of the scriptures which prophesy the advent of the Prophet Muḥammad (see *prophet; the seal of the prophet*). The distortion may take the form of *layy*, which is calculated mispronunciation of words (3:78), or *taḥrīf,* which includes tampering with the text and misinterpreting it (4:46; 5:41). *Ikhfā'* ("concealment"; 5:15) is more comprehensive and covers not only the two types of *taḥrīf,* but also concealment of certain texts from becoming known.

See also: PEOPLE OF THE BOOK, THE.

DIVINATION

Arabic: *istiqsām bi l-azlām.*

5:3 prohibits the practice of divination by means of marked arrows (*azlām*; cf. rabdomancy). The Arabian practice of divination was marked by idolatry and superstition; consequently, any such practice, whether it involves arrows or other instruments, would be covered by the prohibition.

See also: WINE AND GAME OF CHANCE.

DIVORCE

Arabic: *ṭalāq.*

The right of pronouncing divorce essentially belongs to the husband, though the wife may demand divorce.

I. Divorce by Husband. Divorce is to be pronounced thrice, each pronouncement occurring in the non-menstruating days of the woman and only once between two menstrual cycles. After the first pronouncement, the man has the right to take back his wife. After the second pronouncement, if the waiting period (*q.v.*) has elapsed, the couple become separated but may remarry. After the third pronouncement, they cannot remarry, unless the woman is first married to another man who then divorces her (2:230).

During the waiting period, the husband may not turn the wife out of his home, nor must she herself leave (65:1). Upon divorcing his wife, a man must not demand the return of any gifts he might have given her or any property he might have made over to her (2:229). In fact, if he divorces his wife before the consummation of marriage or the determination of the amount of dower (*q.v.*), he must make some kind of payment to her (2:236).

By limiting the number of divorce pronouncements to three, the Qur'ān seeks to reform the pre-Islamic Arabian practice, which gave a man the right to tyrannize over his wife by pronouncing divorce any number of times without having to part with her. By stipulating that divorce be pronounced only when the woman is not menstruating, the Qur'ān intends to eliminate sexual disattraction, a feeling that might arise during menstruation, as a possible cause of divorce. By laying it down that a divorced woman can remarry her former husband only if she has married and received a divorce from another man, the Qur'ān means to make the husband think many times before pronouncing divorce. Finally, the Qur'ān forbids a man to use his influence to prevent his divorced wife from marrying another man (2:232).

II. Divorce by Wife. The divorce, when demanded by wife, is called *khul*ᶜ. A woman who wants a divorce must agree to make some payment to the husband (2:229); the Arabic word used in the Qur'ān for this divorce is *iftidā*', which literally means "to redeem oneself, buy one's freedom."

III. Ẓihār. According to the pre-Islamic Arabian custom, *ẓihār* constituted a divorce. Literally, *ẓihār* is to say to one's wife: "You are to me like the back [*ẓahr*] of my mother," the expression, with its euphemistic use of *ẓahr*, meaning that one shall no longer have sexual relations with one's wife. 33:4 says that such a declaration does not make one's wife one's mother. 58:2–4 lay down the law regarding *ẓihār*. One who commits *ẓihār* must make atonement (*q.v.*) before resuming conjugal relations. He must free a slave; if he lacks the means to do so, he must fast for two months without break; and if he is unable to do even that, he must feed sixty *masākīn* (see *the needy*).

The Qur'ān thus repeals the pre-Islamic customary law in respect of *ẓihār*, according to which *ẓihār* made a wife unlawful to her husband. On the other hand, it regards *ẓihār* serious enough to prescribe atonement for it.

See also: DOUBLE SWEARING; MARRIAGE; OATH OF SEXUAL ABSTINENCE; SUCKLING; WAITING PERIOD, THE.

DIYAH See BLOODWIT

DOUBLE SWEARING

Arabic: **li^{c}ān.*

If a man brings a charge of adultery against his wife, but cannot provide the required four witnesses (see *false allegation of unchastity*), he shall swear by God four times that he is telling the truth, and then say that he invokes the curse of God upon himself in case he is telling a lie; the woman may avert punishment by swearing likewise (24:6–9). This is called *li^{c}ān*, which, literally, is "mutual cursing," but may be translated "double swearing." Since it represents a state of irreconcilable differences, *li^{c}ān* is regarded by Muslim scholars as grounds for the dissolution of marriage.

See also: DIVORCE; FALSE ALLEGATION OF UNCHASTITY; OATH OF SEXUAL ABSISTENCE.

DOWER

Arabic: *ṣaduqah.*

Dower is the husband's marriage gift to the wife. The amount of dower should be specified at the time of wedding, with the dower either to be paid before the consummation of marriage or at a later date. Dower is the right of the wife, who can, if she wishes, exempt the husband from paying it.

One of the words used in the Qur'ān for dower is *ajr* ("remuneration"; 4:24, 25; 5:5; 33:50; 60:10), but it would not to be correct to regard dower as "bride-price," if only because the recipient of the dower is none other than the woman herself. Since, in Islam, it is man who is responsible for founding a family, dower may be interpreted as symbolizing, first, a man's wish to establish the family unit, and, second, his commitment to provide maintenance to the family. The word that brings out best the idea behind dower is *ṣaduqah* (4:4), which carries the connotations of fidelity and truthfulness.

Upon the consummation of marriage, dower must be paid in full, unless the woman voluntarily gives up her right to it. If divorce is pronounced before the consummation of marriage but after the determination of the amount of dower, then the man must pay half of that amount, unless the woman voluntarily decides to forgo it; the Qur'ān recommends, however, that the man pay the dower in full (2:237).

See also: MARRIAGE.

DRESS

Arabic: *libās.*

Dress

I. Functions. Dress has three functions. First, it fulfills a basic physical need: it protects man against the impact of the weather (16:81). Second, it serves a moral function: it covers the private parts of the body (7:26; see also 7:27). When Adam and Eve ate of the fruit of the forbidden tree, they were punished with the loss of their heavenly robes, and, overcome by an instinctive sense of shame, they began to stitch leaves onto their bodies. Third, it gives expression to one's aesthetic sense: dress is *zīnah* ("adornment"; 7:31, 32; see also 7:26), that is, it makes one look good. One of the pagan rites of pilgrimage consisted in circumambulating the Ka^{c}bah (*q.v.*) naked, on the view that the spirit of worship required one to discard all adornment, including dress. The Qur'ān strictly forbade this practice, saying that dress is a *zīnah* with which God has blessed man.

II. Form and Style. The Qur'ān does not prescribe any particular form or style as "Islamic," which means that it leaves the matter of form and style to be determined by climate and individual tastes. It is, however, obvious that, in order to be Islamic, a dress must adequately serve what we have called above the moral function.

III. Spouses as Dress for Each Other. A metaphorical use of the word *libās* may be noted. In 2:187, husband and wife are called "dress" to each other: "they [women] are a dress to you [men] and you are a dress to them." The verse means, first, that the natural relation between husband and wife is that of love, harmony, and mutual support—of the closeness of dress to body—and not, as is sometimes inferred from the story of Adam (2:36), that of hatred or antipathy; and, second, that, by providing sexual satisfaction to each other, the spouses serve to protect each other, like armor—which itself is a kind of dress (16:81; 21:80)—against sexual anarchy.

See also: CHASTITY.

DRY ABLUTION

Arabic: *tayammum.*

Ablution (*q.v.*) must be performed before making *ṣalāt* (*q.v*); in the case of a major impurity (*q.v.*), one must bathe (see *bathing*) before one can perform *ṣalāt.* If, because of the unavailablity or scarcity of water, one is unable to make ablution or bathe, or if one is sick or on a journey, one may make dry ablution, that is, take clean dust and lightly rub one's face and hands up to the wrists (or, on another interpretation, up to the elbows) with it (4:43; 5:6). The Arabic word literally means "to aim [for something]," and to make *tayammum* is to "aim for" clean dust in the above-noted situations.

Tayammum, it might be said, can hardly be called a means of "purification," the stated purpose of ablution and bathing. This is correct. But then the purpose of *tayammum* is not to "purify" the body, but to keep alive a *sense* of purity and maintain respect for *ṣalāt,* so that, even if water becomes available after a long time, one remains disposed to observing the rules for achieving purification and is able to switch to them easily. *Tayammum,* in other words, has a psychological rather than a purificative function.

See also: ABLUTION; BATHING; IMPURITY.

DUᶜĀ See PRAYER

DUNYĀ See EARTHLY LIFE

E

EARTHLY LIFE

Arabic: *dunyā*.

Dunyā (literally, "that which is closer") is "world, worldly existence, earthly life." It is the period during which one is in this world, and it is contrasted with *ākhirah* (see *the hereafter*).

Two apparently conflicting views of earthly life are found in the Qur'ān. On the one hand, a large number of verses present it as something one must take seriously, since it is actions performed in this world that will irrevocably determine one's fate in the next. It is those who lived as believers in this life who will be blessed with good things in the next (7:32). God has created life and death in order to put man to a moral test (67:2). One must, therefore, be constantly mindful of the important consequences that attend upon one's actions. On the other hand, there are verses which present *dunyā* as "play and amusement" (6:32), as being worth no more than "deceptive wares" (3:185). Two poignant pictures of *dunyā* drawn in this vein are to be found in 10:24 and 57:20 (see also 18:45).

The conflict between these two descriptions is easily removed, however. The Qur'ān stresses the importance of earthly life as a seedbed for the next life, and, as such, wants man to take one's conduct in life very seriously. At the same time, it is critical of those who, forgetting that the ultimate abode of man is the next world and not this, devote themselves exclusively to the pursuit of worldly goods and pleasures. It is only when it criticizes people who are deceived by the glamor of this world that the Qur'ān belittles *dunyā*, saying that the next world is infinitely better (2:212; 4:77; 6:130; 7:51; 9:38; 13:26; 29:64; 30:7; 31:33; 35:5; 40:39 47:36; 57:20; 87:16–17), and that one would be foolish to give away enduring happiness for transient pleasures (87:16–17), lasting gain for quick profit (75:20–21; 76:27). The Qur'ān in fact teaches that man must pray for the good things of this world as well as of the next (2:201; 7:156), and that God blesses good people both in this world and in the next (14:27; also 16:122; 29:27).

See also: DEATH; HEREAFTER, THE.

ELECTION

Arabic: *iṣṭifā'; ikhtiyār.*

The Qur'ān contains the notion of election of individuals and nations both; in both cases it is God who elects.

I. Election of Individuals. The election of an individual may signify the bestowing of honor on him for his righteousness; Mary, mother of Jesus, is an example (3:42). More important, it signifies that the individual has been singled out to carry out a special task. Prophets exemplify such election (2:130; 3:33; 20:13). In the first kind of election (Mary), election confers honor on the individual elected; in the second (prophets), election carries with it, in addition to honor, a well-defined responsibility.

II. Election of Nations. The motifs of honor and responsibility are present in the election of nations, but here a third motif, that of trial (*q.v.*), also becomes prominent 44:32–33); trial, in fact, may be called the distinguishing feature of this election. "Trial" implies that a nation has an equal chance of succeeding and failing on the test it is put to. This being so, the election of a nation is "open-ended," that is, it may be annulled if the nation fails to live up to the responsibilities associated with it. Thus, while the Qur'ān contains no examples of an "elected" individual having been stripped of his honor or special status, it contains many examples of nations that were deprived of the distinction once bestowed on them.

EMIGRATION

Arabic: **hijrah, muhājarah.*

I. General. To "emigrate" is to leave one's homeland for another land for the sake of one's religion. Emigration is a distinctly religious act, and that is why the Qur'ān often speaks of it as emigration "in the way of God."

In the early years of Islam, persecution by the Quraysh of Makkah forced the Muslims to emigrate twice, once to Abyssinia (there were in fact two emigrations to Abyssinia, but they may be taken as two phases of the same emigration), and once to Madīnah (in 622), where the emigrants established an Islamic State. While 39:10 anticipates the emigration to Abyssinia and 16:41, 110 refer to that emigration as having taken place, other verses generally bear reference to the Madīnan emigration, which is regarded as the Islamic model of emigration. The following treatment of the subject is offered mainly with that model in view.

II. Emigration as Proof of Faith. Emigration is the last alternative in a Muslim people's struggle to survive and prosper Islamically in a land. When the possibility of Islam's growth, of its very survival rather, in a certain environment, is ruled out and any further effort made in this regard appears to be doomed to failure, an individual or a group of people may decide to leave that environment. When an individual is a member of a regularly formed community and the community decides to emigrate, the individual must emigrate with the community unless he is unable to do so on account of circumstances beyond his control (4:98). Emigration thus becomes a test of faith (4:88-89; 8:74). One who emigrates proves that he is a true believer (8:74–75). As such, he earns the mercy of God (2:218), his sins are wiped off (3:195), and he will get great reward in this world and in the next (9:20; 16:41; 22:58; also 4:100).

III. Legal Entailments. Not only is emigration a praiseworthy act in the eyes of God and one for which great reward is promised, it has certain legal entailments as well. Those who emigrate to another Muslim community are entitled to receive economic assistance from that community (59:8; see *spoils*). Those who do not emigrate may not claim the rights of *walāyah* (*q.v.*) with those in the Islamic State.

IV. Between Despair and Hope. Although emigration is a last alternative, it would not be correct to think of it as an act of despair, for it contains a strong element of hope also—hope that things will turn out better elsewhere. Especially when it takes place on a collective level, emigration becomes a counterpart, in a time of peace, of planned retreat in a time of war.

Above all, however, emigration represents the spirit to sacrifice one's belongings and leave one's dear and near ones for the sake of one's convictions. Many prophets have had to emigrate for the sake of their faith. Abraham is cited (19:47–49; 60:4) as exemplifying emigration in its true spirit and form.

V. Characteristic Feature of the Qur'ānic Concept. The concept of emigration illustrates how the Qur'ān transforms the meanings of ideas it takes over from Arabian culture. A frequently encountered theme in pre-Islamic Arabic poetry is that of willingness to protect one's honor by departing to a far-off place in case living in one's homeland will for some reason bring disgrace to one. For this sense of personal honor the Qur'ān substitutes the sense of the honor of a community founded on a set of religious principles, and, through a "sublimation" of personal feeling into communal commitment, radically changes the nature and purpose of emigration.

See also: WALĀYAH.

ENJOINING GOOD AND FORBIDDING EVIL

Arabic: *al-amr bi l-ma^{c}rūf wa n-nahy ^{c}an al-munkar.*

One of the important injunctions in the Qur'ān is that of enjoining good and forbidding evil (22:41). But first we should look at the terms "good" (*ma^{c}rūf*) and "evil" (*munkar*; cf. article on *evil*) in this expression.

I. Ma^{c}rūf. *Ma^{c}rūf* literally means "that which is familiar, recognized, well-known." As a Qur'ānic term, it stands for a practice that is generally and customarily recognized to be good, wholesome, and reasonable. In its widest sense, *ma^{c}rūf* includes all those acts which establish a relationship of harmony and love between the members of society, e.g. spending in the way of God (*q.v.*) and helping orphans (see *orphan*) and the needy (*q.v.*); the present article deals with *ma^{c}rūf* in this sense. The term also has a narrower meaning, for which see *customary law.*

II. Munkar. Literally "unfamiliar, strange, unrecognized," *munkar* is the opposite of *ma^{c}rūf* and stands for any of those acts which are generally regarded in human societies as reprehensible and reproachful, e.g. pride (*q.v.*), miserliness (*q.v.*), and wrongful appropriation of others' property.

III. Enjoining Good and Forbidding Evil. To enjoin good and forbid evil is, then, an important Qur'ānic injunction. The Prophet is described as enjoining good and prohibiting evil (7:157), and Muslims as a community are made responsible for performing that function (3:104)—performance of the function being part of the *raison d'etre* of their election (*q.v.*) as the median community (*q.v.*; 3:110; see also 9:112 and 31:17). The People of the Book (*q.v.*) are criticized for neglecting the important duty (9:67), though it is admitted that "not all of them are alike," and that some among them persisted in commanding good and forbidding evil (3:114).

See also: GOOD ACTION.

ENVY

Arabic: *ḥasad.*

Envy may lead one to oppose the truth. 2:109 and 4:54 represent some of the People of the Book (*q.v.*) as being motivated by envy in their conduct toward Muḥammad and his followers. 113:5 instructs man to seek God's refuge against the evil envy may cause. While the exhortation is general, implying and covering all types of envy, the verse may be referring more specifically to Satan (*q.v.*), who, envious of the position of preeminence given to man, refused to bow to Adam and vowed that he would try his utmost to mislead man (7:16–17; 17:62; 38:82–83). The title of "envier" in 113:5 would thus belong first and foremost to Satan.

EVIL

Arabic: *sharr.*

The Qur'ān does not deny that evil exists: a man may think that something is good for him, but it may be evil (2:216; also 3:180); man starts to complain as soon as evil touches him (17:83; 41:49, 51); God is quick to show mercy, but slow to inflict evil upon man (10:11), though He uses evil as well as good to put man to the test (21:35; see *fitnah, trial*); the rebellious people shall have an evil abode in the hereafter (22:72; 38:55); and the evil of the Last Day is a dreadful thing (76:7). According to S. 113, God is the only refuge against all types of evil.

And yet evil does not exist in its own right. An important clue to Qur'ānic theodicy is furnished by 113:2: *min sharri mā khalaqa* ("[And say: I take refuge in God] against the evil of what He has created"). The verse does not say "against the evil that God has created," but "against the evil *of* what He has created." This implies that God has created all things essentially for a good purpose, but that He may cause things to have an evil *effect*. Winds and rains, for example, are essentially beneficial, but they were used by God to destroy certain nations. Similarly, man's ignorance of the proper use of something, or his misuse of it, may cause that thing to have an evil effect. Misperception of the true nature of a thing also may result in harm (this explains verses like 2:216 and 3:180). The evil by which man is tried in this world (21:35) is not absolute but relative, in the sense that it constitutes a moral test, thus offering man an opportunity to prove the strength of his moral fiber. In fact, in being a test, evil serves the same function as good; affluence and poverty, for example, may equally be a test for man (21:35) The Last Day, though in some ways evil, is not really so, for on that day the principle of justice—a principle that is eminently good—will reign supreme, and any punishment that is meted out will be meted out in accordance with that principle. Thus, in a wider perspective, all partial evil is seen as universal good.

By denying that evil exists in its own right, the Qur'ān parts company with those dualistic and pluralistic philosophies which set up good and evil as independent forces locked in an eternal conflict with each other.

EXTRAVAGANCE

Arabic: *isrāf*; *tabdhīr*.

Isrāf is "to overdo, commit an excess." The word has a wide range of meanings. "Eat and drink," 7:31 says, "but do not be extravagant" (see also 4:6; 6:141). 25:67 advises one to avoid the extremes of extravagance and niggardliness. 17:33 permits the avenging of murder, but forbids one to oversteps the bounds of the law in doing so. Elsewhere, those who commit excesses in a religious or ethical sense are called "extravagant" (5:32; 10:12; 20:127; 21:9; 26:151; 36:19; 39:53; 40:28, 34, 43; 43:5; 51:34). Pharaoh (10:83; 44:31) and the people of Lot (7:81; 36:19) exemplify such extravagance at its worst.

Tabdhīr has the same meaning as *isrāf* (in the sense of "to be extravagant with one's wealth"), but probably adds the connotation of wantonness; if *isrāf* is excess, *tabdhīr* is sheer and wanton waste.

See also: MISERLINESS; MODERATION.

F

FĀḤISHAH See IMMORALITY

FAḤSHĀ' See IMMORALITY

FAITH

Arabic: *īmān*.

I. General. *Īmān* is the Qur'ānic term for "belief" or "faith" The root *'MN* has the meaning of "peace, security," and *īmān* thus represents the state of being secure in one's belief and of being at peace or harmony with oneself. According to 2:285 and 4:136, the articles of *īmān* are five:

1. Belief in God (see *Allāh*).
2. Belief in the angels (see *angel*).
3. Belief in revealed scriptures (see *kitāb*).
4. Belief in prophets (see *prophet*).
5. Belief in the Last Day (see *the hereafter*).

The relationship between the five articles is as follows: *God* entrusts *angels* with *scriptures* that are to be conveyed to *prophets*, who will then communicate them to mankind so that, following those books, mankind may achieve salvation on *the Last Day*.

II. Faith and Conduct. While it is important to subscribe to the articles of faith, *īmān* also requires that one's conduct reflect one's faith. In other words, one must perform good actions (see *good action; enjoining good and forbidding evil*). The Qur'ān frequently mentions *īman* and good actions together, saying that the two are necessary for salvation. Good actions are thus an index of true *īmān*, and true *īmān* is the ground of good action.

III. Belief in the Unseen. One of the conditions of the right belief is *īmān bi l-ghayb* (2:3). The expression is usually translated "belief in the unseen," that is, belief in God, angels, the afterlife, and other phenomena to which human sensory powers have no access (see *the phenomenal and nonphenomenal realms*).

See also: DISBELIEF; ISLAM.

FALĀḤ See SALVATION

FALSE ALLEGATION OF UNCHASTITY

Arabic: **qadhf.*

Qadhf (literally, "to throw, cast, fling") is to bring a false accusation of unchastity against someone. The word used by the Qur'ān is *ramy*, which has the same literal meaning as *qadhf.*

24:4 requires a person who accuses a "chaste" Muslim woman of adultery to produce four witnesses in support of his accusation, and prescribes a punishment of eighty lashes if he is unable to do so. Although the wording of the verse is, "Those *men* who accuse chaste *women*," Muslim scholars agree that both male and female accusers will receive the same punishment, and that, likewise, it makes no difference whether the accused person is a man or a woman.

Besides stating the punishment of flogging, the verse declares that the testimony of a proven *qādhif* (active participle from *qadhf*) shall never thence be accepted, and that such a man is *fāsiq* (see *fisq*). The verse concludes with a clause of exception: "Except those who repent after that and mend their ways, [to them] God is Very Forgiving, Most

Merciful." This means that *qadhf* is punishable both in this world and in the next, and that a *qādhif* can avert punishment in the hereafter only by repenting sincerely.

See also: DOUBLE SWEARING; MAJOR SIN AND MINOR SIN.

FALSEHOOD

Arabic: *bāṭil.*

Bāṭil means "falsehood." In the Qur'ān the word denotes one or another of several "kinds" of falsehood:

1. False deity: those who call upon any deity other than God call upon *bāṭil* (22:62; also 29:67).

2. Untruth (2:42; 3:71).

3. Wrong path (47:3).

4. Powers or agencies that falsify or distort truth (41:42).

5. Purposeless act or behavior: God has not created this universe without a purpose (3:191; 38:27).

6. Unlawful conduct, such as appropriation of someone's property by wrongful means (2:188; 4:29, 161).

7. That which is liable to be destroyed, thwarted, or undone (7:139; 11:16).

In the struggle between falsehood and truth (*q.v.*), truth is destined to triumph in the end (13:17; 17:81; 21:18; 42:24).

See also: TRUTH.

FAQĪR See NEEDY, THE

FASĀD See CORRUPTION

FASTING

Arabic: *ṣawm, ṣiyām.*

I. General. Muslims are required to observe fasting

during the month of Ramaḍān (*q.v.*). The fast begins at daybreak and ends at sunset. During these hours certain restrictions apply: eating and drinking and sexual intercourse are interdicted. To one who is in a state of *i*^{c}*tikāf* sexual intercourse with his wife is forbidden during the non-fasting hours as well (2:187). *I*^{c}*tikāf* (the Qur'ānic term is ^{c}*ukūf*) is to "retire" to the mosque for a certain number of days in Ramaḍān, devoting oneself to the worship of God.

II. Details of the Injunction. 2:183–185, 187 contain the prescription concerning fasting. These verses were revealed in 2–3 A.H. (624–625 C.E.); vss. 183–184 were revealed first, followed a little later by vs. 185, which in turn was followed by vs. 187. Vs. 183 makes fasting obligatory upon all (i.e. all adult Muslims) but says that a sick person or a traveler may miss fasts, compensating for them later either by fasting—the preferred way, according to vs. 184—or feeding poor people. Vs. 185 revoked the second of these options, leaving fasting the only way for making up for the missed fasts. In *Ḥadīth*, pregnant and nursing women are also allowed to miss the fasts of Ramaḍān and make up for them later, and this permission may be regarded as an amplification of these words in vs. 183: "God wants to make things easy for you, He does not want to make things difficult for you." As for vs. 187, it gives permission to eat and drink and have sexual intercourse during night, that is, during the non-fasting hours, though sexual intercourse during Ramaḍān nights is, as noted above, forbidden if one is in a state of *i*^{c}*tikāf*.

Islam is not the first religion to prescribe fasting for its adherents. According to 2:183, fasting was prescribed by God for earlier peoples also (cf. Zech. 7:3–5 and 8:19). It appears that a "fast of silence" was also observed. Just before the birth of Jesus, Mary observed a fast of silence and refused to speak to anyone (19:26; cf. "Be silent" in Zech. 2:13).

For fasting as one of the ways of making atonement for sins, see *atonement*.

III. Philosophy of Fasting. Fasting—although the word is immediately suggestive of abstinence—is not to be regarded as a practice aimed at inculcating a negative virtue. The principal aim of fasting is to develop and strengthen in man that inner goodness of character from which good action naturally springs. The words *ṣawm* and *ṣiyām* denote a systematic underfeeding of a horse with the purpose of training it to withstand the rigors of war. Fasting, too, is a systematic attempt made to achieve a well-defined goal, that of inculcating spiritual discipline and building moral stamina. The verse that lays down the injunction of fasting (2:183) also states the rationale behind the injunction: "In order that you may achieve *taqwā*"; and *taqwā* (*piety*), which signifies moral restraint or discipline, is presented in the Qur'ān as a prerequisite for good action. Also, according to 2:185, fasting is a means of offering gratitude for the blessing of the Qur'ān, which was revealed during the month of Ramaḍān (see *Qur'ān*).

See also: ATONEMENT; PILGRIMAGE; ṢALĀT; WORSHIP; ZAKĀT.

FAWZ See SALVATION.

FAY' See SPOILS

FIDYAH See ATONEMENT

FIGHTING AGAINST GOD AND HIS PROPHET

5:33 lays down severe punishments for those who engage in *muḥārabah* ("fighting") against God and His Prophet. In the light of the verse itself, "fighting against God and His Prophet" would mean: to declare open war against the social and legal system that has been established in accordance with the injunctions of God and His Prophet. Thus, when acts like highway robbery, arson, murder, and subversion create a problem of law and order in society, the government may give to the criminals involved exemplary punishments, which may include crucifixion and the cutting of hands and feet.

FIRDAWS See HEAVEN

FIRM HANDLE, THE

Arabic: *al-ᶜurwah al-wuthqā.*

"Whoever submits himself to God, being a doer of good deeds, has taken hold of a firm handle" (31:22; also 2:256). That is to say, complete and sincere submission to God furnishes man with true and reliable guidance, guidance that will save him from being misled.

See also: CHORD OF GOD, THE.

FISQ

Fisq (or *fusūq*) is "to commit a transgression or wickedness." In the Qur'ān, however, the word is usually used of a gross violation of the laws of God. Satan committed *fisq* when he disobeyed God (18:50), and so did the peoples of Noah (51:46), Lot (21:74), and Pharaoh (28:32). Those who "do not decide in accordance with what God has revealed" are called *fāsiqūn* (pl. of *fāsiq* [active participle from *fisq*]); 5:47), as are the Hypocrites (*q.v.*; 9:67) and those who falsely accuse others of unchastity (see *false allegation of unchastity*; 24:4). The eating of certain kinds of foods (see *the lawful and the unlawful*) and divination (*q.v.*) are also called *fisq* (5:3; 6:121, 145). The *fāsiqūn* deprive themselves of the ability to receive the guidance of God, and are misled even by those signs of God which lead others to the Right Path (*q.v.*; 2:26; 5:108; 9:24, 80; 63:6). The *fisq* of nations results in their punishment in this world and in the next (2:59; 6:49; 7:165; 10:33; 17:16; 29:34; 32:20; 46:20).

Those who become confirmed in their *fisq* cease to have a position of respect and honor in Muslim society. The news brought by a *fāsiq* must be carefully checked before it is accepted (49:6), and the testimony of those who bring false accusations of unchastity is never to be accepted (24:4).

See also: FUJŪR.

FITNAH

Fitnah has the following meanings in the Qur'ān.

1. *Persecution.* The word is frequently used for the persecution of one person by another or of one people by another (10:83; 16:110; 85:10). *Fitnah* in this sense is termed a greater offense than killing (2:191, 217).

2. *Mischief.* The meaning "to cause to stray from the Right Path (*q.v.*) through guile and mischief" is found in several verses, e.g. 7:27 ("O children of Adam, let not Satan involve you in *fitnah*") and 17:73.

3. *Trial.* God often puts men to the test. The tests may take many forms (see *trial*), but the purpose in each case is the same—to see whether trial brings men closer to God or alienates them from Him. Putting men to the test is a *sunnah* of God (*q.v.*; 29:2), and the good as well as the bad are tried, prophets (e.g. Moses [20:40], David [38:24], and Solomon [38:34]) no less than Pharaoh and his followers (44:17).

4. *Burning.* The wicked shall burn in hellfire (51:13). "Burning," in fact, is the literal meaning of *fitnah*, for the word literally means: to determine the purity of a metal, such as gold, by heating it on fire. The other meanings given above are derived from this one, and the connection between the four meanings is not hard to see. Occasionally, the Qur'ān combines more than one meaning in a single use of the word, as in 51:14 ("Taste your *fitnah*!"), where the word simultaneously means "burning" and "persecution": the wicked used to "persecute" innocent people in the world, in punishment of which they shall be made to "burn" in hell.

See also: CORRUPTION; TRIAL.

FIṬRAH

30:30 reads: "[Follow] the *fiṭrah* on the pattern of which He has created people." In Qur'ānic usage, *fiṭrah* is roughly equivalent to "human nature." *Fiṭrah* is the "natural disposition" of man, and this disposition, 30:30 implies, is essentially good. The Qur'ān seems to suggests that the urge to worship God and serve Him is innate to man. Man is not a *tabula rasa*, but has an instinctive awareness of good and evil (91:8; see *covenant*), though it is up to man to retain that awareness or allow it to become vitiated (91:9–10).

The phrase about *fiṭrah* in 30:30 is preceded by the injunction, "So turn your face in the direction of the [true] religion, with single-minded devotion," and is followed by the comment, "This is the true religion." The verse thus implies that human *fiṭrah* is in accord with the true religion that comes from God, and that religion is not an imposition on man but a response to a call that arises from the depths of *fiṭrah* (see *dīn*). *Fiṭrah* and religion, in other words, complement each other.

See also: COVENANT; DĪN; MAN; REMEMBRANCE.

FLOGGING

Arabic: *jald*.

Flogging is prescribed as punishment for adultery and and false allegation of unchastity (*qq.v.*).

See also: ADULTERY; FALSE ALLEGATION OF UNCHASTITY; PUNISHMENT.

FORGIVENESS

Arabic: *maghfirah.*

God is *ghafūr* ("Very Forgiving"; also *ghaffār* ["Most Forgiving"]). One must never despair of His mercy, for He forgives sins (40:3)—all kinds of sins (39:53). He gives forgiveness to those who believe and do good deeds (5:9; 11:11; 34:4; 35:7; 46:31; 48:29), spend of their wealth in the way of God (64:17), and acknowledge their sins (3:135; 4:110; 28:16). One of the prayers the Qur'ān teaches is that of asking forgiveness of God (2:286; 3:16, 147, 193; 23:118; 73:20; 110:3), and not only for oneself but for others too (3:159; 7:155; 40:7; 59:10; 71:28). The Qur'ān speaks approvingly of, among others, David (38:24), Solomon (38:35), and Jonah (28:16), for they sought forgiveness of God for their lapses. Adam and Eve, too, asked forgiveness of the sin of eating of the forbidden tree, and were forgiven, which incidentally means that, from the Qur'ānic viewpoint, there is no such thing as the original sin.

But while God is Very Forgiving, there is one thing He will never forgive, and that is *shirk* (see *idolatry*). Also, there is no forgiveness for those who disbelieve, prevent people from taking the path of God, and die in a state of unbelief (47:34); commit repeated acts of unbelief (4:137); or are guilty of the heinous sin of hypocrisy (see *the hypocrites*).

Since God is Forgiving, He likes men to cultivate the attribute of forgiveness and be forgiving to other human beings (24:22; 64:14).

See also: REPENTANCE.

FORNICATION See ADULTERY

FREEDOM AND DETERMINISM

Does man possess freedom of the will or are his actions predetermined by God? The Qur'ān treats the issue not from a metaphysical standpoint (something Muslim theologians forgot, with grave consequences for Muslim theology), but from a practical viewpoint. A brief background is necessary.

I. Root of the Problem. The problem of freedom and determinism has its root in the conflicting results yielded by man's experience of the external world. On the one hand, man has a strong feeling of freedom; he sees that he can make a plan and execute it. This feeling is at the bottom of man's endeavor to improve his situtation in the world and is the driving force behind all progress. Also, in his interaction with other human beings in society, man develops a sense of rights and responsibilities with respect to other people, and this sense presupposes freedom of action. On the other hand, man has a strong feeling that his power to act is limited. He builds a house and a tornado levels it to the ground. Right when he is ready to reap the harvest, a disaster strikes and he feels helpless. Since these two types of experiences are among the most fundamental that man has, it would be unwise, in attempting to solve the problem of freedom and determinism, to wish either of the two types of experiences away and seek exclusive support for the free-willist or the determinist thesis.

II. Qur'ānic Perspective. Instead of denying either of the two kinds of experiences, the Qur'ān confirms both, striving only to correct the imbalance of outlook that might arise on the one or the other side. On the free-willist side the imbalance arises as a result of pride. Intoxicated by political or economic power, man sometimes acts as if he is a law unto himself, as if he is not accountable to anyone for his actions. Whether he actually believes or not that he is completely free to do what he likes and has unrestricted power is immaterial; he probably does not, for it would be absurd to do so. But this is not the concern of the Qur'ān. The Qur'ān's concern rather is with the practical behavior of man. If a man conducts himself in such a way *as if* he is not subject to a higher power, *as if* he were a law unto himself, the Qur'ān takes notice and warns that man is not beyond God's reach, that God can at any moment seize him and punish him. Wherever it stresses the point that God has absolute power, the Qur'ān does not mean to deny that man has any power, but to deny that man is so powerful as to defy God with impunity. In many Makkan sūrahs, the wealthy Quraysh are criticized for their haughty attitude, and 90:5 says: "Does he [man] think that no one shall have any power over him?"

Imbalance on the determinist side takes the form of fatalism or of an attempt to deny moral responsibility. While pride leads to a virtual denial of a higher law, fatalism leads to a concession of the existence of such a law, but imputes to that law such compulsive power as to absolve man of all responsibility, especially for evil actions. When this happens, the Qur'ān again takes notice, rejecting the plea of "not guilty." 6:148 reports the Idolators (see *idolatry*) as saying that they could not have committed idolatry had God wished otherwise. 6:149 seems to support the Idolators' plea when it says that had God wished He would have guided all human beings. But 6:150 eliminates the apparent contradiction by pointing out that it is base desires (see *hawā*) that make a man a candidate for misguidance by God. God allows such a person to become misguided, which means that the plea of "not guilty" (made in 6:148) does in fact stand refuted.

III. Facilitation, Sealing, and Accountability. This brings us to a consideration of several ideas. The first of these is "facilitation." According to some Qur'ānic verses (e.g. 16:93), God guides whomever He likes and misguides whomever He likes; according to others (e.g. 18:29), it is up to man to choose guidance or misguidance. There is, however, no contradiction between the two sets of verses. 92:5–10 say that God facilitates (*taysīr*) the doing of good actions for those who would perform them, and that he facilitates the doing of evil actions for those who would do such actions. Since the "facilitation" in each case comes from God, God may be regarded as having guided or misguided. But insofar as it is man who, through his attitude and conduct, asks for the one or the other kind of facilitation, man is responsible for his actions.

The same point is made in those verses (e.g. 2:7) which speak of God's sealing up of the hearts of men. The sealing (*q.v.*) takes place in accordance with the law of God (see *sunnah of God*) that those who become steeped in sin do not deserve to be guided by God, and, as a result, are deprived of the ability to come to the Right Path (*q.v.*; 61:5). Ultimate power thus belongs to God, and if He gives man a certain amount of freedom, He does not to that extent forfeit His omnipotence, for He has the power to take away from man the freedom He has given him. In fact God has already put constraints on that freedom. The birth and death of an individual, for example, are preordained (6:2; 57:2), the individual being responsible for what he does in the period between his birth and death.

The question of freedom and determinism in the Qur'ān is not divorced from the ideas of trial (*q.v.*) and accountability (*q.v.*). According to the Qur'ān, man is not tried beyond his capacity (2:286), i.e. he is to be held accountable only to the extent that he has freedom. In view of this, it would be preposterous to think that (to paraphrase a Persian verse) God would tie a man firmly to a board, cast him into the sea, and command him not to get wet. If the idea of trial has to have any meaning, the idea of responsibility must follow, and if the idea of responsibility is not to become a complete mockery, the idea of freedom of the will must follow. Among the simplest and clearest verses in the Qur'ān is this: "So he who wants to believe may do so, and he who wants to disbelieve may do so" (18:29; also 17:15). The following verse needs no comment either: "God does not change the condition of a people until that people [first] changes its own condition" (13:11; also 8:53).

IV. Conclusion. If the Qur'ānic perspective on the issue of freedom and determinism is kept in mind, a conflict between divine omnipotence and human freedom would hardly arise. The mostly sterile discussions of the problem by Muslim theologians of early centuries were a result of the disregard of the context in which the Qur'ān raises the issue and treats it.

See also: ACCOUNTABILITY; ALLĀH; TRIAL.

FUJŪR

Fujūr is "impiety, wickedness, evil." The word is used in the Qur'ān antonymically to *taqwā* (see *piety*; 38:28; 91:8), and thus connotes throwing moral restraint to the winds. Man has been given an instinctive sense of *fujūr*, just as he has been given an instinctive awareness of *taqwā* (91:8).

See also: FISQ; TAQWĀ.

FURQĀN See CRITERION, THE

FUSŪQ See FISQ

G

GAME OF CHANCE See WINE AND GAME OF CHANCE

GHANĀ'IM See SPOILS

GHAYB See PHENOMENAL AND NON-PHENOMENAL REALMS, THE

GHĪBAH See BACKBITING

GHUSL See BATHING

GIVER OF GOOD TIDINGS

Arabic: *bashīr*, *mubashshir*.

I. Common Use. Every prophet (*q.v.*) gives to his people the good tidings that they will achieve success and salvation if they follow the message he has brought from God (2:213; 4:165; 6:48; 18:56).

II. Special Use. In 61:6 the word *mubashshir* is used specifically of Jesus, who, according to the verse, announced that there would be come after him a prophet called Aḥmad—another name of Muḥammad. According to some Qur'ān commentators, the kingdom of heaven of which Jesus spoke was none other than the perfect social order that Muḥammad brought into existence, that social order being an earthly replication of the heavenly kingdom to be established in the next life.

See also: WARNER.

GLORIFICATION OF GOD

Arabic: *tasbīḥ, taqdīs.*

The heavens and the earth and all things in them glorify God (17:44; 57:1; 59:1, 24; 61:1; 62:1; 64:1). The angels glorify Him (7:206; 21:20; 39:75; 42:5), and so does thunder (13:13; see also 21:79; 34:10; 38:18). Everything, however, glorifies God in its own way, and we may not be able to understand the exact mode of its glorification (17:44). In some verses (20:130; 50:39–40; 52:48–49; 76:26) *ṣalāt* (*q.v.*) is called "glorification," since glorification of God is the essence of *ṣalāt.*

GOD See ALLĀH

GOOD ACTION

Arabic: *ṣāliḥ* (pl. *ṣāliḥāt*); *ḥasanah* (pl. *ḥasanāt*); *iḥsān.*

Faith and good actions are so often mentioned together in the Qur'ān (e.g. 2:25, 62, 82, 277; 3:57; 5:69; 18:88; 20:82; 25:70; 34:37; 40:40; 64:9; 65:11) that one cannot help thinking that the Qur'ān regards the two as integrally related. Faith, the Qur'ān seems to be saying, should necessarily lead to good action, and good action must naturally spring from faith.

What are the good actions? Although one can, on the basis of specific Qur'ānic statements, provide some kind of a list (which would then include acts like: worshipping the One True God, telling the truth, helping the poor), a convenient way to describe a good action is to say that it is the carrying out of a commandment of God with the sincere intention of earning the pleasure of God. In other words, it is not simply a question of performing certain actions, but is also a matter of the attitude with which one performs them.

Good actions will not fail to win reward from God (9:120; 11:115; 12:56, 90). In fact, they will be rewarded manifold (see *reward*), as opposed to evil actions, which will receive only proportionate punishment (see *punishment*). Also, good actions wipe off bad actions (11:114; 29:7; 64:9).

See also: ENJOINING GOOD AND FORBIDDING EVIL.

GOOD LOAN

Arabic: *qarḍ ḥasan.*

Wealth spent in the way of God and for His sake is called the "good loan." "Good" implies that the wealth is spent generously and not with a view to making a worldly gain. Wealth so spent is regarded by God as a "loan" which He will repay manifold (2:245; 57:11, 18; 64:17).

The term "good loan" is general enough to cover anything spent in the way of God in accordance with the above-stated conditions. In a more specific sense, it refers to wealth given in order to meet communal needs and exigencies, ranging from taking care of orphans to financing a war. The obvious context of 2:245 and 57:11 is war. In 57:18 and 64:16–17, where it is distinguished from *ṣadaqah* (*q.v.*), and in 5:12 73:20, where it is distinguished from *zakāt* (*q.v.*), "good loan" stands for the wealth given to meet special communal needs.

The good loan helps wipe off one's sins and earns one forgiveness and salvation (5:12; 64:17).

GRATITUDE

Arabic: *shukr.*

As the recipient of numberless blessings from God,

man owes gratitude to Him (2:172; 8:26; 16:14, 78; 27:19; 46:15), though most people are not grateful (2:243; 10:60; 12:38; 27:73; 34:13; 40:61). The Qur'ān presents *shukr* as the most natural feeling that can arise in a thinking human being. The universe in which man finds himself is so geared to man's use and benefit that it points to the existence of a bountiful God. Recognition of the bountifulness of God thus generates, or ought to generate, a feeling of gratitude in man (see S. 1).

Some verses (2:158; 4:147; 35:30; 42:23; 64:17) describe God as being *shākir* or *shakūr* (active participles from *shukr*). The meaning is that God "appreciates" the good work of human beings. If he appreciates such work, then it follows that He will give reward for it. "Appreciation," in fact, is the essential meaning of *shukr*, "gratitude" also being a form of appreciation.

Another word used for "gratitude" is *ḥamd*, though a more accurate translation of it would be "grateful praise." The word, which is almost exclusively used with God as the object of *ḥamd* (e.g. 1:2; 6:1, 45), occurs mostly in exclamatory expressions (*al-ḥamdu li llāhi* ["Grateful praise is due to God alone!"]). In some verses (e.g. 20:130; 50:39) *ṣalāt* (*q.v.*) is equated with *ḥamd* (and glorification [*q.v.*]) since the essence of *ṣalāt* is the offering of gratitude and praise to God.

GREETING

Arabic: *salām*.

Salām ("peace") is the Islamic greeting, the complete greeting being *salāmun* (or *as-salāmu*) *ᶜalaykum* ("peace be upon you"; 6:54).

Salām is one of the watchwords of Islam (*salām* and "Islam" [*q.v.*] are from the same root), and constitutes part of the etiquette Islam teaches its followers. One of the names of God is *salām* (59:23) which means that He is the source of true peace.

Salām must be offered upon meeting one another or entering someone's house (6:54; 24:27, 61; also 11:69; 15:52; 51:25). Upon being greeted with *salām*, one ought to return a "greeting that is better than that or comparable to it." In the hereafter, those who earn paradise (see *heaven*) will be greeted with *salām* upon entering it (16:32), and they themselves will greet one another with this greeting (10:10; 25:75; 56:26; also 33:44).

According to 33:56, Muslims must send greetings of peace upon Muḥammad, the form being: *ṣallā llāhu ᶜalayhi wa sallama* ("may God have mercy upon him [Muḥammad] and give him peace"). Muslims usually do so whenever they take the name of Muḥammad, though, technically, it would suffice for one to do so once in his lifetime.

GUIDANCE

Arabic: *hudā*.

One of the prayers a Muslim utters several times a day in *ṣalāt* (*q.v.*) is that for guidance: "Guide us to the Right Path" (1:5).

I. Source of Guidance. Guidance comes from God, the only source of guidance (2:120; 7:178; 10:35; 17:97; 18:17). God, however, has not compelled man to accept guidance, but, having shown him the right and wrong paths, has left him free to make his choice (76:3; see *dīn*). The divine guidance for mankind is mediated through prophets (42:52; 79:19), who are the prime examples of the rightly guided (6:84–90). Man's ultimate fate in the next world depends on how he responds and reacts to the guidance that comes to him from God.

II. Forms. Divine guidance takes several forms:

1. *Instinctual Guidance.* "He who created everything, then gave [it] guidance." Everything has been provided with guidance appropriate to its being and nature. Thus every animal follows the instincts peculiar to it. Man, too, possesses guidance at the instinctual level: "Then He imbued it [human self] with [an instinctive sense of] its evil and its good" (91:8).

2. *Rational Guidance.* As a rational being, however, man needs more than instinctual guidance. By endowing him with reason, God has enabled man to reflect on the external universe, and also on his own being, and thus arrive at certain conclusions about his position and role in the world.

3. *Revelatory Guidance.* Finally, God has provided man with unmistakable guidance in the form of revelation (*q.v.*). The Torah and the Evangel are called guidance (3:3–4), and the Qur'ān is described as furnishing the best guidance (17:9).

Needless to say, all these forms of guidance complement each other, and, possessing all of them, man has no excuse to abandon the path of truth.

See also: COVENANT; MISGUIDANCE.

H

ḤABL ALLĀH See CHORD OF GOD, THE

ḤABL AN-NĀS See CHORD OF GOD, THE

ḤABṬ AL-AᶜMĀL See NULLIFICATION OF DEEDS

ḤADĪD See IRON

HADY See SACRIFICE; SYMBOLS OF GOD

ḤAJJ See PILGRIMAGE

ḤALF See OATH

ḤALLĀF See OATHMONGER

ḤAMD See GRATITUDE

ḤĀMĪ See ANIMAL VENERATION

ḤANĪF

Ḥanīf (pl. *ḥunafā'*) is one who worships God with single-minded devotion. Abraham is called *ḥanīf* and is praised for being one. The Qur'ānic use of the word, with reference to Abraham, seems to stress two things. The first is rejection of idolatry: Abraham was a *ḥanif*, and he was no idolator (2:135; 3:67, 95; 6:79; 16:123). The second is avoidance of factionalism or parochialism: Abraham was a *ḥanīf*, and not a Jew or Christian (2:135; 3:67). In other words, Abraham distinguished himself in worshipping the One God with complete devotion and undivided loyalty. Muḥammad is asked to take Abraham as his model and become a *ḥanīf* (16:123; also 10:105; 30:30), and his followers are instructed to do the same (2:135; 3:95).

ḤAQQ See TRUTH

ḤĀQQAH See HOUR, THE

ḤARĀM See LAWFUL AND THE UNLAWFUL, THE; SACRED LANDMARK, THE; SACRED MONTHS, THE; SACRED MOSQUE, THE

ḤASAD See ENVY

ḤASANAH See GOOD ACTION

HAWĀ

Hawā ("base desires") is one of the principal causes of misguidance (*q.v.*). Etymologically, the word implies a "falling off." *Hawā* is thus a falling off from the desired standard of conduct, and the use in 7:176 gains its full force only when the etymology of the word is kept in mind. Also, there may be a connection between *hawā* and *hāwiyah* (the "pit" into which the people of hell will "fall"), one of the names of hell (*q.v.*). In 23:71 an ontological dimension is added to the meaning of the word: "If the truth were to follow their [disbelievers'] *ahwā'* [pl. of *hawā*], the heavens and the earth would have been destroyed, and also those who are in them."

Hawā, or preoccupation with one's whims and caprices, gives rise to pride, and pride in turn may lead to rejection of the truth (2:87) and opposition to justice (4:135). The Prophet does not speak from *hawā* (53:3), which means that the scripture he presents is not the product of his own imagination but is a revelation from God (53:4). There are people who set up their *hawā* as their "deity" (25:43), and such are deservedly misguided by God (45:23; see *misguidance*), their hearts being sealed up by God (47:16; see *sealing*).

See also: MISGUIDANCE; SEALING.

HEAVEN

Arabic: *jannah.*

Heaven is the abode of the righteous and virtuous in the next life. The Arabic word *jannah* means "garden"; *firdaws* (18:107; 23:11) is "paradise." Heaven was the original but temporary home of Adam and Eve, who, after they had discovered their strengths and weaknesses in their encounter with Satan (*q.v.*), were despatched to earth, where they were supposed to endeavor, through moral action, to win their original home, namely, heaven, which then onwards would be their eternal home (25:15). That is why heaven is described as a place the good shall "inherit" (7:43; 19:63; 26:85; 43:72). The good, that is to say, shall become rightful heirs to Adam and Eve.

I. Description. Heaven is as vast as the heavens and the earth (3:133; 57:21). It is a garden with streams of water flowing in it (2:25; 3:15, 136, 195, 198; 5:85, 119; 9:89; 10:9; 57:12; 61:12). It is a place of bliss and happiness (36:55; 69:21–22; 88:8–10) and of peace (6:127; 10:25), so that its residents shall have in it whatever they desire (16:31; 41:31; 43:71), and shall be free from all fear and regret (7:49)—fear of any calamities befalling them in the future and regret for things done in the past. In heaven, people will wear silk and armbands of gold and pearls (35:33; 76:12). 55:46–76 give a fairly complete picture of heaven and its pleasures.

There are, it seems, several "types" of heaven, meant for different categories of people. S. 55 gives a description of two heavens (vss. 46–60), and follows it up with a description of two others (vss. 62–76), hinting that the latter are "less" in rank (*dūn*) than the former. The distinction would seem to correspond to the distinction made in S. 56 between the two categories of the residents of heaven: 56:10–26 (people who always took the lead in performing good actions) would thus correspond to 55:46–60, and 56:27–40 to 55:62–76.

II. Conditions for Entering Heaven. Certain conditions have to be fulfilled before one can enter heaven: faith and performance of good actions (2:25, 82; 4:57; 29:58; 65:11), obedience to God and His Prophet (48:17), a life lived in piety (38:49–50; 44:51–52; 51:15; 52:17; 54:54; 68:34), and steadfastness shown in the tests (see *trial*) to which God puts man in this world (2:214; 3:142; also 9:111). Mere association or affiliation with a certain group or people is not a passport to heaven (2:111).

See also: BARZAKH; DEED-SCROLL; HELL.

HELL

I. Names. Hell is the abode of the evil and the wicked in the afterlife. The names most frequently used for hell are *nār* ("fire") and *jahannam* ("Gehenna"). Other names are: *ḥarīq* ("conflagration"; 3:181; 8:50; 85:10), *ḥuṭamah* ("crusher"; 104:4–5), *saᶜīr* ("flames"; 22:4; 31:21; 42:7; 67:10), and *hāwiyah* ("pit"; 101:9).

II. Description. The Qur'ān contains graphic descriptions of what will happen in hell. Hell is an "evil place" (3:197; 14:29; 25:34, 66), and being in hell is "the great humiliation" (9:63). Hell has seven gates, a certain group of people destined for each (15:44). Its fire will burn forever and will be fanned the moment it begins to die down (17:97). As soon as it receives a batch of people, it will roar and bellow, bursting with rage (67:7–8). Those in hell will be the fuel of hell (2:24; 21:98; 66:6; 72:15). Chained to tall pillars(104:9), they will be surrounded by torment on all sides, receiving punishment "from above their heads and from under their feet" (29:55; also 23:104), their faces buffeted by fire (23:104), the fire even leaping onto their hearts (104:7). As soon as their skins are eaten away by the fire, they will be supplied with new skins (4:56). They will cry for death but will be denied it (43:77; also 35:36), so that they will neither live nor die (20:74); their punishment will not be commuted either (40:49–50; 43:75). Their food shall consist of filth (69:36), thorny bushes (88:6), the fruit of the zaqqūm tree (see *the accursed tree*), and they shall have hot and pus-filled water to drink (14:16; 38:57; 55:43; 78:21). Those who hoard up gold and silver and refuse to spend of it in the way of God will have their foreheads, sides, and backs branded with the same gold and silver (9:35). There are several regions in hell, and the hypocrites (*q.v.*) shall be in the lowest region (4:145).

The people of hell will continually bicker and argue. Those who listened to their evil leaders in the world will charge them with misleading them, while the leaders will exonerate themselves of all responsibility (34:31–33; also 38:64; 50:27–28).

See also: BARZAKH; DEED-SCROLL; HEAVEN.

HELPERS, THE

Arabic: *anṣār*.

The name *anṣār* (9:100, 117) is used of the Madīnan Muslims who, upon the arrival of the Makkan emigrants in 622 (see *emigration*), offered them full support (8:72, 74), helping them become established in the new environment.

The aid of the Helpers was crucial in the establishment of Islam and Muslims in Madīnah.

See also: DISCIPLE; EMIGRATION.

HEREAFTER, THE

Arabic: *ākhirah*.

I. The Concept. *Ākhirah* (also: *al-yawm al-ākhir* ["the Last Day"] and *ad-dār al-ākhirah* or *dār al-ākhirah* ["the Last Abode"]) represents the notion that man does not perish with his death but shall have another life (see *death*). The main components of the concept of *ākhirah* (which is contrasted with *dunyā* [*q.v.*]) are resurrection, judgment, and recompense. On an appointed day God will resurrect the dead, judge them according to their deeds, and send the righteous to heaven (*q.v.*) and the wicked to hell (*q.v.*). The proceedings of the Day of Judgment are summed up in 39:68–75.

II. Description. The Qur'ān uses many names to describe the Last Day—most of the hundred or so names given by Ghazālī are taken from the Qur'ān, each name describing a certain aspect or feature of that day. The following may be noted: *al-yawm al-ḥaqq* ("the true [inevitable] day"; 78:39); *al-yawm al-maw*^{c}*ūd* ("the promised day"; 85:2); *yawm al-wa*^{c}*īd* ("the day of threat"; 50:20); *yawm al-qiyāmah* ("the day of resurrection"; 2:85; 3:55; 4:109; 5:14; 6:12; 17:97; 28:41; 39:15; 75:6); *yawm al-khurūj* ("the day of exodus [from graves]"; 50:42); *yawm at-tanādī* ("the day of mutual calling [as a result of panic]"; 40:32); *yawm al-jam*^{c} ("the day of assembling" [of all people, for the purpose of judgment]; 42:7); *yawm at-talāqī* ("the day of meeting"; 40:15); *yawm al-ḥisāb* ("the day of reckoning"; 38:16, 53; 40:27); *yawm al-faṣl* ("the day of distinction" [between the good and the evil]; 37:21; 44:40); *yawm ad-dīn* ("the day of recompense"; 1:3; 15:35; 37:20; 38:78; 56:56); *yawm at-taghābun* ("the day of winning and losing"; 64:9); *yawm al-*

khulūd ("the eternal day"; 50:34).

III. Possibility, Necessity, and Certainty. That resurrection is possible is suggested by the pattern of resurrection which marks the created world and which man witnesses every day (30:19, 24, 50; 43:11; 50:11). Moreover, if God was able to create man—in fact the whole universe—the first time, it should be so much easier for Him to re-create him a second time (36:79, 81; 46:33).

That the hereafter is not only possible but necessary is suggested by the fact that the present world is not the world where complete recompense for good or bad actions can be given. Good actions often go unrecognized, and evil actions often go unpunished. It is, therefore, morally necessary that there be another world where good and evil can be fully recompensed and all accounts settled in strict accordance with the principle of justice.

That the hereafter is not only possible and necessary but will actually take place is known through the revelation brought by prophets. Some prophets (e.g. Abraham [2:260]) were actually shown how God would revive the dead in the hereafter (see also 2:259, where an unnamed righteous man is given a similar demonstration).

IV. Conclusion. Belief in the hereafter is one of the three fundamental Islamic tenets, the other two being monotheism (*q.v.*) and prophecy (*q.v.*). From the Qur'ānic point of view, the hereafter constitutes a vindication of God's justice and wisdom, and it is probably for this reason that 2:28 equates disbelief in the hereafter with disbelief in God.

See also: ACCOUNTABILITY; BARZAKH; DEATH; DUNYĀ; HEAVEN; HELL; HOUR, THE; RECOMPENSE.

ḤIBR

Ḥibr (pl. *aḥbār*) is "scholar," i.e. a Jewish scholar of the Law. The Qur'ān praises those *aḥbār* (and *rabbāniyyūn* [see *rabbānī*]) who judged in accordance with the Torah

(5:44) and criticizes those who, neglecting their duty as moral guardians of society, did not forbid people to amass wealth in unlawful ways (5:63), being guilty of the practice themselves (9:31).

See also: MONASTICISM; QISSĪS; RABBĀNĪ.

HIJRAH See EMIGRATION

ḤILF See OATH

ḤISĀB See ACCOUNTABILITY

HOLY LAND, THE See BLESSED LAND, THE

HOLY SPIRIT, THE

Arabic: *ar-rūḥ al-qudus.*

The "Holy Spirit" is the spirit that comes from God as an aid or succor to certain chosen people of God, especially prophets. The expression is used for Gabriel, as can be seen from 16:102. The verse says that the Qur'ān was conveyed to Muḥammad by the Holy Spirit, and since the angel Gabriel brought the revelation (2:97), Gabriel would be the Holy Spirit. Elsewhere Gabriel is called *ar-rūḥ al-amīn* ("the Trustworthy Spirit"; 26:193), or simply *ar-rūḥ* ("the Spirit"; 78:38; 97:4). Jesus was aided by the Holy Spirit (2:87, 253; 5:110).

HOUR, THE

Arabic: *sā^{c}ah.*

"The Hour" means "the hour of resurrection" (see *the hereafter*). It is described as impending (42:17; 54:1), as a certain and inevitable happening (*ḥāqqah*; 69:1–3), and as a fateful and terrible event (54:46). Only God knows when the Hour will come (7:187; 31:34; 33:63; 41:47; 43:61, 85), though it will come all of a sudden (6:31; 12:107; 22:55; 33:63; 43:66; 47:18), which means that one must be in a state of constant moral readiness.

See also: HEREAFTER, THE.

HUDĀ See GUIDANCE

ḤUDŪD ALLĀH See PRESCRIPTIONS OF GOD

HUE OF GOD, THE

Arabic: *ṣibghat Allāh.*

2:138 exhorts Jews and Christians to assume the *ṣibghah* ("hue, color") of God, for, the verse asks, whose *ṣibghah* is better than God's? The verse, in other words, enjoins them to rise above religious factionalism and offer true obedience to God. The expression contains an allusion to the Jewish and Christian rites of baptism (the Arabic for "baptism," *iṣṭibāgh*, is from the same root as *ṣibghah*).

ḤUKM See ARBITRATION

HUMAN NATURE See FIṬRAH

HUNTING See ATONEMENT; IḤRĀM; LAWFUL AND THE UNLAWFUL, THE

HYPOCRITES, THE

Arabic: *munāfiqūn* (sing. *munāfiq.*)

I. General. The "Hypocrites" were those Madīnans who, upon noticing the growing strength of Islam, had converted to Islam, but only in order to safeguard their interests. Since they lacked true conviction, they were ready to switch loyalties whenever they saw Islam in danger or felt that supporting Islam would mean making sacrifices or suffering losses. They did not realize that true honor and power belong to God and His Prophet (63:8). For their despicable behavior, the principal motives of which were love of worldly gain (9:58) and fear of death (3:168), the Qur'ān threatened them with punishment, saying that they would be consigned to the lowest region of hell (4:145). 9:80 says that even if Muḥammad were to ask forgiveness for them seventy times, God would not forgive them (see also 63:6).

II. Their Tactics. Since they were converts of expediency, the Hypocrites looked for opportunities to undermine Islam, and on different occasions used different tactics to accomplish their ends. The Qur'ān criticizes them for spreading rumors at a time of crisis or emergency (33:61), enjoining evil and forbidding good (9:67; see *enjoining good and forbidding evil*), refusing to fight with Muslims against the latter's enemy (3:167; 33:13), offering assistance to forces hostile to Islam (59:11), and using their loud professions of faith to shield their sinister designs (63:1–2). The Hypocrites try to deceive God, but in fact they deceive no one but themselves (4:142). The Prophet is instructed to fight not only the disbelievers but also the Hypocrites (9:73).

III. Muḥammad's Attitude toward Them. Stern action against the Hypocrites was taken only later; for both religious and political reasons it was not advisable to crush them right after they had been identified. From a religious point of view, formal profession of faith is sufficient to include a man in the fold of Islam and he cannot be excluded from it until he commits acts that categorically and unmistakably brand him a hypocrite. From a political point of view it was inadvisable to take action against them at an early stage because Muslims were weak at that time. Muḥammad, therefore, waited until the actions of the Hypocrites had fully exposed them. Once they were thus exposed, they were cut off from the community of Muslims.

I

ᶜIBĀDAH See WORSHIP

IBLĪS See SATAN

ᶜIDDAH See WAITING PERIOD, THE

IḌLĀL See MISGUIDANCE

IDOLATRY

Arabic: *shirk; ishrāk.*

I. Meaning. The literal meaning of *shirk* (and *ishrāk*) is "association, partnership," and it is used in this sense in 34:22; 35:40; 46:4. Technically, it means "idolatory," that is, the act of associating with God other beings and objects, or that of setting up partners to Him. One who commits *shirk* is a *mushrik* (pl. *mushrikūn*), a term that is often used in the Qur'ān to designate the idolatrous Arabs, who may accordingly be called "Idolators" (with a capital I).

II. Critique of Shirk. The Qur'ān criticizes *shirk* in all forms it might take, whether representational (statues and images; 6:74; 14:35; 53:19–20; 71:23), creedal (belief that beings other than God partake of God's essence or attributes; 6:100;7:191–192; 13:16), or behavioral (serving or offering obedience, in practice, to powers or beings other than God; 6:136–138; 17:64).

According to the Qur'ān, *shirk* has no foundation. God is the Creator and as such the sole Sovereign of the universe (6:101, 164; 10:68; 17:111; 25:2). Furthermore, deeply embedded in the human soul is the recognition that there is only One God; at times of crisis idolators forget all other deities and call upon God only (6:40, 63; 10:22; 29:65). Had there been two deities, the universe would have been destroyed (21:22).

III. Unforgiveable Sin. *Shirk* is the most heinous of the major sins (see *major sin and minor sin*; 4:48; 31:13). Any good actions a *mushrik* might have done will be of no avail to him in the hereafter (*q.v.*; 6:88; 9:17; 39:65; see *nullification of deeds*). *Shirk* is the one sin that God will never forgive (4:48, 116); paradise (see *heaven*) will be absolutely denied to a person who is guilty of this sin (5:72). A Muslim may not marry a *mushrik* person (2:221); he may not even pray for a deceased *mushrik* (9:113). As for Abraham's prayer for his idolatrous father (26:86), he made it because he had promised his father that he would do do; but when he realized that his father was an "enemy of God," Abraham washed his hands of him (9:114).

IV. Shirk and Adultery. The Qur'ān subtly likens *shirk* to adultery (*q.v.*; 24:3). In committing adultery a person wrongfully associates someone with his lawful sexual partner; in committing *shirk*, one wrongfully associates other deities with God.

See also: ANGEL; LAWFUL AND THE UNLAWFUL, THE; MONOTHEISM; RIGHT PATH, THE.

IḌṬIRĀR See NECESSITY

IFTIDĀ' See DIVORCE

IGHTIYĀB See BACKBITING

IGNORANCE, AGE OF See AGE OF IGNORANCE

IḤRĀM See PILGRIMAGE

IḤSĀN See GOOD ACTION

IḤṢĀN See CHASTITY; MARRIAGE

IKHFĀ' See DISTORTION OF SCRIPTURE

IKHTIYĀR See ELECTION

ĪLĀ' OATH OF SEXUAL ABSTINENCE

ILḤĀD See BLASPHEMY

ĪMĀN See FAITH

ĪMĀN BI L-GHAYB See FAITH

IMHĀL See RESPITE

IMLĀ' See RESPITE

IMMORALITY

Arabic: *faḥshā', fāḥishah.*

Etymologically, *fāḥshā'*, or *fāḥishah,* carries the twin notions of "excess" and "foulness," and is applied to obscene and indecent acts. The following are called *fawāḥish* (pl. of *faḥshā'*) by the Qur'ān: adultery (*q.v.*; 4:19, 25; 17:32); homosexuality (7:80; 27:54; 29:28; 33:30; 65:1); marrying the wife of one's father (4:22); slander (24:16–17). Those who avoid *fawāḥish* may expect the forgiveness of God (42:37; 53:32).

The Qur'ān enjoins Muslims to avoid immorality in all

its forms, glaring and subtle (6:151; 7:28, 33; 16:90). Immorality is forbidden by God (6:151; 7:33) but encouraged by Satan (*q.v.*: 2:169; 24:21). If one has committed an act of immorality, one must remember God, ask forgiveness for the sin, and resolve not to commit such an act again (3:135). *Ṣalāt* (*q.v.*) is especially effective in preventing man from committing immorality (29:45).

See also: ADULTERY; CHASTITY.

IMPURITY

Arabic: **janābah.*

Impurity is of two kinds, minor and major. Minor impurity is caused by relieving nature, and is removed by means of ablution (*q.v.*); major impurity is caused by sexual intercourse (4:43), or nocturnal emission, and is removed by means of bathing (*q.v.*). Under certain circumstances either kind of impurity may be removed by means of dry ablution (*q.v.*).

2:221 forbids sexual intercourse with a menstruating woman—menstruation being regarded as an impurity—but allows it after the woman has bathed.

See also: ABLUTION; BATHING; DRY ABLUTION.

INFANTICIDE

Arabic: *wa'd.*

Some Arabian tribes practiced infanticide, and the Qur'ān abolished the practice, at the same time seeking to reform the mentality behind the practice.

I. Motives. The principal motives behind the practice were two: fear of poverty and fear of disgrace. The first motive is referred to in 6:151 and 17:31, which forbid one to kill one's children from fear of becoming destitute, saying that it is God Who provides sustenance to all.

As 81:8–9 suggest, it was usually baby girls who were

killed. Here the second motive also comes into play. Defeat in battle meant capture of the tribe's women by the enemy. An Arab poet says that his tribe fights valiantly because it knows that, if it loses the battle, its "fair-complexioned beauties" would be distributed among the enemy troops and humiliated by them.

II. Deeper Cause. These motives themselves can be explained by reference to the notion of woman as a liability. Woman, it was thought, had no substantial contribution to make toward her tribe. Being weak and vulnerable herself, she could not defend the tribe in a time of crisis. She had to be brought up in gold and silver, only to be married off—a sheer waste of wealth. The *human* worth of woman was hardly recognized, and the only worth she had (besides being the idealized subject of love poetry) was to be measured in terms of her material contribution to the tribe she belonged to. This view of woman is reported in 43:17–18: "And when one of them is given the good news of [the birth of] a daughter, his face turns dark and he chokes with anger, [saying] 'What, is it the one who is to be raised in jewelry and who is incompetent in confrontation?'"

III. Qur'ānic Reform. The Qur'ān tackled the problem using its characteristic ethico-legal approach. On the legal plane, it declared the killing of a human being (without cause or justification) an unlawful act that earned one capital punishment in this world (5:32; 17:33) and eternal punishment in hell (4:93). On the ethical level, it repeatedly said that God alone is the Sustainer, that it is God Who provides for all human beings.

INFĀQ See SPENDING IN THE WAY OF GOD

INHERITENCE, LAW OF

I. Function and Purpose. By contributing toward an equitable distribution of wealth in society, the Qur'ānic law of inheritance seeks, on the one hand, to reduce the possibility of concentration of wealth, and, on the other, to eliminate some of the major causes of conflict, wrong, and injustice in society. Like the other economic prescriptions of the Qur'ān, such as *zakāt* (*q.v.*), the basic aim is of the law of inheritance is to achieve social justice and harmony.

The rules of inheritance are given in 4:11–12, 176 (see also 4:7); they are called God's "command" (*waṣiyyah*; 4:12), and also the "prescriptions of God" (*q.v.*), observance of which will be rewarded with paradise (see *heaven*), and violation with hellfire (4:13–14). Here it is not necessary to give details of those rules, but a brief statement of the principles underlying the law of inheritance may not be out of order.

II. Principles.

1. The property is to be divided rather than kept intact. Thus systems like primogeniture are ruled out.

2. The property is to be distributed among ascending as well as descending relatives. This reflects the Qur'ānic view of the family as an extended unit.

3. Females as well as males shall succeed to property. The idea here is that physical strength, the supposed distinction of the male and the supposed guarantee of protection of the family or clan, shall not be the sole criterion of eligibility for inheriting. For the same reason, minors and invalids inherit, and they cannot be deprived of their shares on grounds of age or physical handicap.

4. The male will get a double share as opposed to the single share of the female. This is in keeping with the requirement that the responsibility for providing maintenance to the family lies with the male, who, accordingly, is entitled to a greater share.

5. No wills may be made in favor of a designated heir, i.e. one whose share has been stated in the Qur'ān. Also, the amount bequeathed may not exceed one-third of the property. (See *bequest.*)

6. The distribution of the estate will take place after the testamentary provisions have been enforced and any outstanding debts paid.

See also: BEQUEST.

INIQUITY

Arabic: *ẓulm.*

I. Range of Meanings. Iniquity (the Arabic word means "injustice, wrong, denial of a right") is a term that covers many kinds of sins and crimes: idolatry (*q.v.*; 31:13); disbelief (*q.v.*; 2:254); rejection of the verses of God (6:21, 157; 7:37; 10:17); passing judgments in accordance with the law of other than God (5:45); violation of the "prescriptions of God" (*q.v.*; 2:229; 65:1); commission of grossly immoral acts (see *immorality*; 29:31); forcibly preventing people from worshipping in mosques (2:114); ridiculing and name-calling (49:11).

II. Punishment. While God accepts the repentance (*q.v.*) of those who sincerely resolve to become good (5:39), those who are steeped in *ẓulm* shall not be guided by God (9:19, 109; 14:27; 46:10; 62:5) or achieve salvation (6:21, 135); rather, they will receive punishment in this world (6:45; 7:162, 165; 10:13; 11:67, 94; 18:59; 23:27; 27:52; 28:59) and in the next (10:52; 11:113; 21:29; 34:42; 43:65).

III. Ẓulm against Oneself. Since every action will be recompensed in the hereafter (*q.v.*; see also *recompense*), the *ẓulm* committed by one will recoil upon one, bringing on one the punishment that goes with it. It is in this sense that the Qur'ān says that wrongdoers ultimately bring harm to themselves (2:57; 3:117; 7:160; 9:70; 10:44; 11:101; 16:33, 118; 29:40; 30:9; 43:76).

See also: JUSTICE.

INSĀ' See ABROGATION

INSĀN See MAN

INSPIRATION See REVELATION

INTERCALATION

Arabic: *nasī'*.

Nasī' literally means "to push away." The word is used, for example, for the act of pushing a camel away from the watering-place. Technically, it refers to the pre-Islamic practice of "shifting" the otherwise fixed sacred months (*q.v.*). Fighting was forbidden during these months, but the Arabs, if they wanted to continue a war into a sacred month or saw an opportunity of raiding or plundering another tribe during this period, sometimes violated that law, later compensating for the violation by treating a non-sacred month as sacred. The Qur'ān calls this practice an "increase in disbelief" (9:37).

INTERCESSION

Arabic: *shafā^{c}ah*.

Several verses in the Qur'ān negate the idea of intercession on the Last Day (2:48, 123, 254). According to several other verses, those who think that, in the hereafter, intercessors will save them from being punished for their evil deeds will be disabused of their false notions on the Last Day (6:94; 7:53; 26:100; 30:13; 74:48). All such verses imply that, on the Last Day, the principle of just recompense will be strictly enforced and one will have to bear full consequences for one's actions.

But there are a few verses which suggest the possibility of intercession in the hereafter. 20:109 says that no one will be able to intercede on anyone's behalf except with the permission of God, and 21:28 leaves open the possibility of making intercession for an individual for whom God gives the permission. According to 43:86, only he who bears true witness shall be able to make intercession. These statements seem to contradict those cited earlier. Can the contradiction be resolved?

It goes without saying that the very idea of an intercession that violates the principle of justice is anathema to the Qur'ān. After all, if intercession could save those from punishment for whom, according to the Qur'ān itself, there is no salvation, then the Qur'ān has been guilty of a blatant self-contradiction. But then does the Qur'ān allow for intercession at all? Is it possible to permit intercession without upsetting the principle of justice? One of the situations in which, according to Iṣlāḥī, this may be possible is, when the good and bad deeds of an individual are evenly matched and the individual, strictly speaking, is on the "borderline" between heaven and hell. The permission to make intercession in such borderline cases, and then in accordance with the conditions stated above, would not amount to a violation of justice, but may in fact be regarded as a manifestation of divine mercy and as a bestowing of honor on those who are allowed to make intercession.

See also: ANGEL.

INTEREST

Arabic: *ribā*.

Ribā literally means "increase, increment, addition." As a technical term it is usually explained as: a fixed increment that a creditor receives from the debtor on the capital he has loaned to the latter for a certain period of time. In 30:39 the word is used for the capital that is lent for the purpose of taking interest on it. The Qur'ān forbids the taking of interest (2:278; 3:130; also 4:161). It contrasts interest on the one hand with *ṣadaqah* (*q.v.*), saying that God causes *ṣadaqah* to "grow and prosper" but "smothers" interest (2:276), and on the other hand with the profit made in business (2:275), this profit, as against interest, having been earned in a legitimate manner.

2:275 describes the psychology of the interest-charging money-lender: love of interest makes him crazy, so that on the day of resurrection he will appear to have been touched by the devil and, as a result, to have lost his senses.

See also: ṢADAQAH; ZAKĀT.

IQTIṢĀD See MODERATION

IRON

Arabic: *ḥadīd.*

In 57:25 ("And We sent down iron, which carries great power and [other] benefits for people") "iron" means "power, might"; to be more specific, it means political power and military might, since the basis of such power or might is iron, i.e. weapons made of iron. Since physical force can be an important means of establishing justice and equity on earth, iron, as a symbol of that force, is potentially a blessing. It is for this reason that, though extracted from the earth, iron is described in the verse as having been "sent down" by God. The blessing of iron, like other blessings, ultimately comes from God, and the words "sent down" point to the source of the blessing. The "other benefits" of iron are the social and civilizational uses of iron.

IRTIDĀD See APOSTASY

ISLAM

I. Meaning. The word "Islam" (properly, "Islām") has the twin meanings of "submission" and "peace." "Submission" means submission to God, and it is total and unconditional submission that is signified. "Peace," too, is to be construed in a comprehensive sense: peace in personal life and peace in social life. The two meanings are interconnected in that submission to God is supposed to result in peace in the life of the individual and in that of society.

II. Islam, Perennial and Historical. Historically speaking, Islam is the name of the religion that made its advent in Arabia 1400 years ago and is associated with Muḥammad, and the word is used in this sense in, e.g., 5:3; 9:74; 49:17. But the other revealed religions were also "Islam" in that they, too, embodied the idea of submission-cum-peace; thus Abraham and other prophets are described as being the followers of Islam (2:128, 131–133; 3:67; 12:101). From this point of view, historical Islam becomes only the latest manifestation of perennial Islam. The two meanings are so blended in the Qur'ān that sometimes (e.g. 3:19, 85) it becomes difficult to decide which meaning is primarily intended, or whether only one meaning is intended. In some verses (e.g. 3:83) the whole universe is described as *muslim* (see below), in the sense that it "obeys" or "submits" to God. The implication of such verses is that man, too, should submit to the God Who is obeyed by the whole universe.

III. Beliefs, Rituals, and Code of Conduct. Islam is a set of beliefs, a set of rituals, and a code of conduct.

1. *Beliefs.* The fundamental Islamic beliefs are three: belief in the oneness of God (see *Allāh; monotheism*), belief in the hereafter (*q.v.*), and belief in prophecy (*q.v.*) A Muslim is also required to believe in angels (see *angel*) and in all heavenly scriptures (see *kitāb*).

2. *Rituals.* There are four principal rituals: *ṣalāt* (*q.v.*), *zakāt* (*q.v.*), *ṣawm* (see *fasting*), and *ḥajj* (see *pilgrimage*).

3. *Code of Conduct.* Islam lays down a code of conduct for man's life. The Qur'ān contains prescriptions dealing with the various spheres of human life, social, political, economic, legal, and moral, which have been discussed in various articles in the present work.

IV. Īmān and Islam. What is the relationship between *īmān* ("faith" [*q.v.*]) and Islam? From a literal point of view, *īmān* stands for "assent, admission, acknowledgment," and "Islām" for "compliance, capitulation, obedience." As such, the locus of *īmān* is the heart, whereas the locus of "Islam" is one's whole physical and spiritual being, and to be a "Muslim" (active participle from "Islam") signifies not only making acknowledgment in one's heart but also giving proof of that acknowledgment through one's conduct. As such, "Islam" is more general and comprehensive than *īmān*. The Qur'ān, however, uses the two words sometimes as if they were synonyms (as in 10:84 and 51:35–36) and sometimes as if they were different (as in 49:14). The Qur'ān, it seems, recognizes them as formally different but otherwise integrally related to each other.

See also: DĪN; FAITH.

ISRĀF See EXTRAVAGANCE

IṢṬIBĀGH See HUE OF GOD, THE

IṢṬIFĀ' See ELECTION

ISTIKBĀR See PRIDE

ISTIQSĀM BI L-AZLĀM See DIVINATION

ISTIWĀ' ^{c}ALĀ L-^{c}ARSH See THRONE

I^{c}TIKĀF See FASTING

IZĀGHAH See SEALING

J

JAHANNAM See HELL

JĀHILIYYAH See AGE OF IGNORANCE

JALD See FLOGGING

JAM^{c} BAYN AL-UKHTAYN See MARRIAGE

JANNAH See HEAVEN

JĀR AL-JUNUB, AL- See NEIGHBOR

JĀR DHŪ L-QURBĀ, AL- See NEIGHBOR

JAZĀ' See RECOMPENSE

JIBT

Jibt literally means "a thing of no use," and is used of idols, soothsayers, magicians (see *magic*), and so on. To believe in *jibt* (5:51), therefore, is to believe in powers and agencies that, according to the Qur'ān, lack reality or substance. A rough English equivalent would be "superstition."

See also: MAGIC.

JIHĀD

I. Meaning and Forms. The literal meaning of *jihād* is "to strive." Technically, *jihād* is any endeavor that is made to further the cause of God, whether the endeavor is positive (e.g. promoting good) or negative (e.g. eradicating evil) in character, takes the form of social action or private effort, involves monetary expenditure or physical struggle, or is made against the enemy without or the enemy within (i.e. against "the bidding self" [*q.v.*]). The reduction of *jihād* to "war" is thus unjustified, though war is an important form of *jihād*, and a number of Qur'ānic verses about *jihād* (e.g. 8:74, 75; 9:44) refer primarily to fighting. The comprehensive nature of *jihād* is evidenced by such verses as 29:69: "Those who strive in Us [=Our way], We guide them to Our ways." When *jihād* takes the form of war, it is known as *qitāl* ("fighting").

II. Jihād in the Way of God. One's *jihād* should be "in the way of God" (5:35; 9:41), i.e. one should engage in *jihād* with the sole purpose of pleasing God and not with the aim of winning personal or national glory. The expression also implies that one's personal attachments, business interests, etc., must not prevent one from undertaking *jihād* (9:24), for the cause of God must take precedence over all other causes. Furthermore, it is not enough simply to "strive" but to strive to the utmost. 22:78 says, "Strive in the way of God to the best of your ability [literally, the way the striving should be done]." Those who strive in the way of God, putting at stake their lives and their wealth may expect to receive the mercy of God (2:218), and shall have a greater reward than those who "sit back" (4:95). Willingness to fight in the way of God marks a true believer (8:74, 75; 49:15) off from an unbeliever (see *disbelief*) and a hypocrite (see *the hypocrites*; 9:44, 86).

See also: CIVIL WAR.

JINN

I. Nature and Constitution. The *jinn* are an order of creation with fire as their constitutive element (7:12; 15:27; 38:76; 55:15). They have extraordinary powers; one of the *jinn* in Solomon's court offered to bring the throne of Queen Sheba before Solomon could blink his eyes (27:39).

II. Morally Responsible Beings. As is clear from S. 55, the *jinn* are, like humans, morally responsible beings; like humans, they possess freedom of the will and will be recompensed for their actions in the hereafter (*q.v.*). According to S. 72 (which bears the name *Jinn*), there are good *jinn* and evil *jinn* (vs. 14). 6:130 suggests that, like humans, the *jinn* have their own prophets (see *prophet*), whose message they are supposed to accept and follow.

III. Relationship with Human Beings. The Qur'ān specifies (18:50) that Satan (*q.v.*) was a *jinn*. By refusing to bow to a creature of dust, he disobeyed God and became "one of the disbelievers." Expelled from heaven (*q.v.*), he swore revenge: he would make a relentless effort to misguide man (7:16–17; 15:39; 17:62). Satan and his followers thus attempt to mislead men; obviously they could do so only by establishing some kind of contact with men. And since the *jinn* have extraordinary powers, evil men, too, are keen to seek their help in thwarting the truth (72:6). Every prophet has been opposed by evil *jinn* and humans (6:112), but God protects prophets against the satanic horde (22:52). There are thus limits to what humans and *jinn* can accomplish through collaboration; they cannot, for example, produce the like of the Qur'ān (17:88; see *Qur'ān*). But foolish men have often regarded the *jinn* as possessors of knowledge of the *ghayb* (see *the phenomenal and non-phenomenal realms*; 34:14), and have even worshipped them (34:41).

See also: ANGEL; EVIL; PHENOMENAL AND NON-PHENOMENAL REALMS, THE; PROPHET; SATAN.

JUSTICE

Arabic: *ᶜadl, qisṭ.*

The Qur'ān upholds justice as an absolute value: "God commands [the doing of] justice . . ." (16:90). 5:8 says: "Hostility toward a people must not induce you to be unjust [toward it]; be just; [for] that is closer to piety [*q.v.*]" (see also 4:58; 5:42; 49:9).

4:3 says that if one has more than one wife, one must treat all of them fairly, otherwise have one wife (see also 4:129).

See also: INIQUITY.

K

KA^{c}BAH

The Ka^{c}bah, a cube-like structure ("Ka^{c}bah" and "cube" are etymologically related) in the city of Makkah, is the principal sanctuary of Islam and the center of activity during the annual pilgrimage (*q.v.*).

See also: ANCIENT HOUSE, THE; PILGRIMAGE; SACRED MOSQUE, THE.

KABĪRAH See MAJOR SIN AND MINOR SIN

KAFFĀRAH See ATONEMENT

KHALĪFAH See CALIPH

KHAMR See GAME OF CHANCE AND WINE

KHĀTAM AN-NABIYYĪN See SEAL OF THE PROPHETS, THE

KHATM See SEALING

KHAYṬ AL-ABYAḌ, AL- See WHITE STREAK, THE

KHAYṬ AL-ASWAD, AL- See WHITE STREAK, THE

KHIYĀNAH See BREACH OF TRUST

KHUL[c] See DIVORCE

KITĀB

I. Meanings. *Kitāb* (pl. *kutub*) has a number of meanings.

1. Scripture or revealed book: 2:177, 285; 3:79; 4:136.

2. Authoritative document: 37:157.

3. Record, that is, the book that contains a complete record of everything (6:59; 50:4)—also called the Preserved Tablet (*q.v.*; 85:22).

4. Deed-scroll (*q.v.*).

5. Decree, that is, a decision made by God (8:68).

6. Law or injunction (2:235; 98:3).

7. Letter or epistle (27:28, 29).

Sometimes the word oscillates between two or more meanings, as in 66:12, where it may belong to (1) or (6) or both, or as in 34:44, where it may belong to (1) or (2) or both. At any rate, all the meanings, including (5) and (6), are interrelated, the basic meaning of "something written" supplying the unifying link.

II. Kitāb as Scripture. The most important meaning of *kitāb*, of course, is "scripture, revealed book." *Kitāb* in this sense may include other meanings. Scripture takes the form of a message or epistle from God (6), is an authoritative document (2), and is a collection of divine prescriptions (5). *Kitāb* often means the Torah (2:44, 85, 87, 101, 113, 121; 3:23), which was *the* revealed Book before the Qur'ān; in the expression "People of the Book" (*q.v.*) also, "the Book" is the Torah. In 2:2 the Qur'ān is called "The Book."

Belief in scriptures is one of the articles of Islamic faith (see *faith*).

See also: DEED-SCROLL.

KUFR See DISBELIEF

KURSĪ See THRONE

L

LA^cNAH See CURSE

LAW OF INHERITANCE See INHERITANCE, LAW OF

LAWFUL AND THE UNLAWFUL, THE

Arabic: *ḥalāl* ("lawful"); *ḥarām* ("unlawful"); *taḥlīl* ("to declare something lawful"); *taḥrīm* ("to declare something unlawful").

I. General. The "lawful" is that which a person may have or make use of; the food one may eat is "lawful," and the women a man may marry are "lawful." That which a person may not have or make use of is "unlawful."

The Qur'ān attaches great importance to the question of the lawful and the unlawful. It often discusses the subject together with that of monotheism, implying that true belief in the oneness of God demands that man abide by God's commandments regarding what is lawful and what is not, and that God alone has the right to declare something lawful or unlawful.

As a rule, the Qur'ān, instead of providing a list of things that are lawful, enumerates things that are unlawful, by implication declaring the rest lawful. Hence the principle: everything is lawful and permissible unless there is an injunction to the contrary (see 6:119). The principle is supported by verses like 2:29, which says that God has created everything for man's use, and 2:168, which permits one to eat the good things of the earth.

II. Details. The subject of the lawful and the unlawful is a vast one, and reference to some of its aspects is made in other articles in this work. In the following paragraphs the subject is treated with reference to food and matrimony.

1. Food. 5:96 declares sea animals lawful, and the general form of the declaration implies that sea animals are lawful food whether they are found dead and eaten or are caught live and then killed.

With reference to animals of the land, 6:145 puts the following on the forbidden list: carrion, blood outpoured, swineflesh, flesh of an animal slaughtered in the name of other than God. To these four things 5:3 adds another six, but these are only extensions of the four things mentioned in 6:145. Thus *munkhaniqah* ("dead through strangling"), *mawqūdhah* ("dead through hitting"), *mutaraddiyah* ("dead through falling"), *naṭīḥah* ("dead through butting"), and "the animal a predator has eaten of" are all extensions of "carrion," while "the animal slaugthered at a *nuṣub*" (a "spot" or "place" consecrated to an idol [pl. *anṣāb*]; 5:3, 90) is an extension of "the animal slaughtered in the name of other than God." As for the lawful animals, their flesh may be eaten after they have been properly slaughtered. Proper slaughtering, called *tadhkiyah* (5:3) includes the taking of God's name, and only His name, over the animal (6:118). Animals may also be hunted for food, either with hunting instruments (5:94) or trained animals (5:4). The animal killed by a hound is lawful food provided one has taken God's name over the animal and the hound has not eaten of the animal's flesh but has saved it for its master (5:4).

Wine-drinking is prohibited (see *wine and game of chance*).

5:5 allows Muslims to eat the food of the People of the

Book (*q.v.*). This, however, is not a permission to eat foods otherwise declared unlawful by the Qur'ān.

2:173 allows the eating of forbidden food in case of necessity (*q.v.*).

2. Matrimony. 4:22–24 forbid a Muslim man to marry the following women:

a. Mother.

b. Daughter.

c. Sister.

d. Paternal aunt.

e. Maternal aunt.

f. Brother's daughter.

g. Sister's daughter.

h. Mother by suckling.

i. Suckling sister.

j. Mother-in-law.

k. Step-daughter (if she has been brought up by one and one has consummated marriage with her mother).

l. Real son's wife.

m. Two sisters (i.e. having two sisters in marriage at the same time; Arabic: *jam^{c} bayn al-ukhtayn*).

n. Married woman, unless she is a war captive.

The basic principle underlying the prohibition to marry these women is that one's relations with one's immediate female relatives—mother, daughter, and sister—should be based on pure kindred feelings and not on sexual love; this explains (a), (b), and (c). Women who are so closely related to one as to be virtually like one's mother, sister, and daughter are also unlawful; this explains (d) through (l). Having two sisters in marriage is prohibited because of the likelihood that jealousy will create feelings of hostility between them. The principle underlying this prohibition finds an extension in *Ḥadīth*, which forbids one to have in marriage, at the same time, a woman and her aunt, or a woman and her niece.

Certain other extensions of the prohibition to marry

the women listed above may be taken to be understood, e.g. that it is unlawful to marry not only one's mother but also the mother of one's mother, and not only one's daughter but also the daughter of one's daughter.

4:3 permits a Muslim man to marry up to four women at the same time, but stipulates that he must treat them equally and fairly, otherwise have one wife (see also 4:129).

4:24 says that it is lawful for a man to marry women other than those described in 4:23–24, but stipulates two conditions for the validity of marriage with them: *iḥṣān* and dower (*q.v.*). *Iḥṣān* is "to take someone under one's care or protection," and the condition means that one should marry a woman with the intention of providing her protection on a permanent basis. In other words, marriage is an enduring relationship and so arrangements like temporary marriage are ruled out.

2:221 forbids one to marry idolatrous women. 5:5 allows a Muslim male to marry a Jewish or Christian woman. A Muslim woman, however, is not permitted to marry any non-Muslim (see *marriage*).

Having permitted marriage, the Qur'ān forbids adultery (*q.v.*).

See also: DIVORCE; MARRIAGE; WINE AND GAME OF CHANCE.

LAWḤ MAḤFŪẒ See PRESERVED TABLET, THE

LAYLAT AL-QADR See NIGHT OF DECREE, THE

LAYY See DISTORTION OF SCRIPTURE

LESSER PILGRIMAGE, THE See PILGRIMAGE

LIᶜĀN See DOUBLE SWEARING

LIBĀS See DRESS

M

MAGHFIRAH See FORGIVENESS

MAGIC

Arabic: *siḥr.*

I. Is Magic Real? S. 20 describes the contest between Moses and Pharaoh's magicians. The magicians cast their ropes and sticks, and "the next moment it appeared to Moses as if their ropes and sticks were in motion" (vs. 66) The words "appeared . . . as if" suggest that magic does not alter phenomenal reality, but only affects one's perception of it. In other words, magic is illusion.

But a few Qur'ānic verses give the impression that magic may not be entirely without reality. In 2:102, satans (i.e. evil *jinn* [*q.v.*] and evil humans [see *Satan*]) are described as having developed the science of magic, which science the Israelites, in the period of their religious and moral decadence, avidly pursued (cf. Isa. 47:9, 12–13). Also, 114:4 teaches one to pray for God's refuge against the evil of the "knot-tying women," or sorceresses.

The apparent contradiction between 20:66 and 2:102 is removed if we take illusion to be one of the ways in which magic achieves its effect. 7:116 says that, in performing their magic (called "trick" in 20:69), Pharaoh's magicians "cast a spell on the people's eyes." Like 20:66, it implies that not reality but one's perception of it is changed by magic. As for 114:4, it is not necessary to take it as proof of the reality of magic, for the verse may be a caricature of magicians at work. It may accordingly be said that much of what passes under the name of magic the Qur'ān would regard as a hoax. Since it calls magic "disbelief" (2:102), the Qur'ān obviously forbids the practice of magic.

II. Charge of Sorcery against Prophets. According to 51:52, one of the stock charges brought against prophets (e.g. Moses [7:109; 26:34; 40:24]; Jesus [5:110]) was that they were magicians or sorcerers. The charge referred to the miracles (see *miracle*) performed by the prophets (e.g. 43:49), and was made by people in full knowledge of the fact that miracles are different in kind from magic (27:13).

Muḥammad, too, was called a sorcerer by his Makkan opponents (10:2). Since Muḥammad performed no miracles, at least not in the sense in which the word is normally understood, what does the charge mean? 43:30 says that Muḥammad's opponents rejected the "truth" by calling it *siḥr*, and the next verse reports their demand that the Qur'ān should have been revealed to one of the notables of Makkah or Ṭā'if. The two verses thus provide a clue to the answer: it was the Qur'ān, with its great persuasive power, that was called "sorcery"; Muḥammad, in other words, was regarded as composing a discourse that "spellbound" his listeners and had a "magical" effect on them.

See also: JIBT; MAJOR SIN AND MINOR SIN; MIRACLE.

MAḤRŪM See NEEDY, THE

MAJOR SIN AND MINOR SIN

Arabic: *kabīrah* ("major sin"; pl. *kabā'ir*); *ṣaghīrah* ("minor sin"; pl. *ṣaghā'ir*).

I. Distinction. The Qur'ān divides sins into two

broad categories, major and minor. Although it nowhere provides detailed lists of the two types, the Qur'ān makes it sufficiently clear what sins it would place in which category. Generally speaking, all those acts which have been explicitly declared by the Qur'ān (and the *Sunnah*) to be unlawful, have been threatened with grave punishment in this world or in the next, or in both, and constitute an open defiance of the Islamic religion or a flagrant violation of a religious commandment would be major sins, other sinful acts being minor sins.

II. Types of Major Sins. Major sins themselves may be divided into several types. The following categorization is adapted from Ghazālī. The worst of all major sins are obviously disbelief (*q.v.*) and idolatory (*q.v.*). Next in gravity are acts which constitute offenses against life and against the institution of the family, which guarantees the perpetuation of the human race; such acts are murder (5:32), adultery (*q.v.*), and homosexuality (7:80; 27:54; 29:28; 33:30). The next category consists of acts of wrongful appropriation of property, and these are: theft (5:38), usurping the property of orphans (4:10), and receiving interest (*q.v.*; 2:278–279). A final category of major sins would include wine-drinking (see *wine and game of chance*), false allegation of unchastity (*q.v.*), practice of magic (*q.v.*; 2:102), and fleeing from the battlefield (8:16). According to *Ḥadīth*, bearing false witness and being undutiful to one's parents are also major sins.

III. Intention. While it is possible to make a formal distinction between major and minor sins, the intention with which a sinful act is committed may change the status of that act. For even a minor sin, if committed with the intention of defying God or making a mockery of religious commandments, becomes a major sin because it then constitutes a challenge to the sovereignty of God. In general, however, the distinction between the two types of sins holds, and 4:31 says that if one avoids the major sins, God will forgive him his minor sins (see also 42:37; 53:32).

MALAK See ANGEL

MAN

Arabic: *insān*.

I. Origin of Man. Like everything else in the universe, man was created by God. The heavens and the earth existed before man was brought into being, and so did angels (see *angel*) and *jinn* (*q.v.*). The first man was Adam (Arabic: Ādam), the name referring to the "terrestrial" nature of man, and that in two senses: first, earth is the constitutive element of man, and, second, in the whole universe it is the earth that is the natural place for man to inhabit and is ideally suitable for the development of his physical, mental, and spiritual faculties (see 2:36).

II. Distinction of Man. 51:56 describes ᶜ*ibādah*—worship of God (see *worship*)—as the purpose of the creation of man (and of the *jinn*). But man, instead of being forced to worship or offer obedience to God, has been left free to make his choice between obedience and disobedience (see *freedom and determinism*). In other words, he has been given freedom of the will. Here a question arises. According to the Qur'ān, angels and *jinn* are also "rational" beings and, as such, possess freedom of the will. What, then, was distinctive about man? Angels, although they could disobey God if they so willed, are so pure of nature that in practice they do not disobey Him (see 66:6). The *jinn* not only can disobey God, they have a history of disobedience to God; Satan (*q.v.*) was a *jinn* (18:50). It appears, however, that the *jinn* possessed only a limited amount of freedom, and that man was the first to be endowed with a great amount of it, enough freedom for him to deserve the title of the "caliph" (*q.v.*) of God. As such, the creation of man represented the greatest experiment the universe was ever to witness. Man being the chief protagonist in this drama, the heavens and the earth were made subject to him (31:20; 45:13; see *nature*) and the angels and *jinn* were both commanded to prostrate themselves before man. Man was thus given a position of preeminence in the scheme of things (17:70), and it was against this position that Satan protested (17:62).

III. Nature and Psychology of Man. Morally, man is capable of telling good from evil and choosing the one over the other. God has given him a sense of what is good and evil (91:8; see *covenant, fiṭrah*), thus leaving him free to work out his own destiny. Essentially, man is disposed toward good, though Satan's successful deception of him in Eden showed that man has his weak points: false hopes and promises can lure him, and his base desires (see *hawā*) and wishful thinking can be exploited by his enemy. But his vulnerability is offset by his ability to mend his ways. Adam, after he had sinned, sought forgiveness and was forgiven (2:37). Incidentally, since Adam was forgiven by God, man is not regarded as laboring under any original sin.

Intellectually, man is capable of distinguishing between truth and falsehood. He is capable of rational action, and, in presenting its message before him and urging him to accept it, the Qur'ān makes repeated appeals to human reason (2:73, 164, 242; 3:118; 13:4; 16:12, 67; 21:10; 23:80; 24:61; 30:28; 45:5; 57:17).

Temperamentally, man is liable to become somewhat smug and impatient. If he becomes affluent, he seldom gives thanks, taking his good fortune for granted, though he is quick to fret and complain if he falls on hard times (10:12; 11:9; 17:67, 83; 39:8, 49; 42:48; 70:19–21; 100:6). Pride makes him contentious (18:54). There is in him an element of recklessness. When he is threatened with punishment for disobedience, he arrogantly asks for the punishment to be precipitated (17:11; 21:37). Forgetting his lowly origin (75:37), he often becomes rebellious and denies the truth

(16:4; 36:77). But these statements should not be construed to mean that the Qur'ān is pessimistic about man. Qur'ānic criticism of man is frequently criticism of a certain group of people, e.g. the Makkan opponents of Muḥammad. This is borne out by the fact that the Qur'ān often draws exceptions to the type of statements cited above, a good example being 70:22–34. The essential Qur'ānic view of man is that he is a being with opposing tendencies (see *the bidding self; the censorious self*), and that he has the ability to understand, and control, the dialectical relationship that exists between these tendencies.

See also: BIDDING SELF, THE; CENSORIOUS SELF, THE; FIṬRAH; FREEDOM AND DETERMINISM; NATURE.

MANIFEST PROOF

A manifest proof is one that establishes the truth in an unmistakable way; it can take the form of a scriptural statement, a piece of reasoning, or a miracle performed by a prophet. Several words are used:

1. *Bayyinah.* A *bayyinah* is a "distinctly clear proof." A prophet, having perceived the truth in its indubitable form, is in possession of a *bayyinah* (6:57; 11:17, 28, 63, 88), and it is *bayyināt* (pl. of *bayyinah*) that he presents before his people (6:157; 5:32; 7:73, 85, 105; 35:25), though, unfortunately, the latter's stubbornness makes them deny the undeniable and develop differences with regard to the truth (2:203; 3:105; 10:13; 40:22; 98:4). In 47:14 the word is used of conscience: the voice of conscience is clear and unmistakable for those who would heed it.

2. *Burhān.* A *bayyinah,* despite its clarity, may be disregarded by one who is presented with it, but not so a *burhān,* which compels attention, though one may still reject it out of pride or obstinacy. Moses, when he was sent to Pharaoh, was given two *burhāns*, those of turning his staff into a serpent and turning his arm completely white upon drawing it out of his bosom (28:31–32). In 12:24 the word *burhān* is used for the compelling power that the conscience of a good man has over him; Joseph is saved from committing adultery by a *burhān* "he saw from his Lord" (12:24; cf. *bayyinah* in 47:14). Those who claim that one must be either a Jew or a Christian in order to achieve salvation are asked to present a *burhān* in support of their belief (2:111), as are those who worship deities other than God (21:24; 23:117).

3. *Sulṭān.* A *sulṭān* is a decisive proof that renders one's opponent completely helpless. Etymologically, the word may have, besides the well-known meaning of "overwhelmingness," the additional meanings of "hugeness" and "sharpness." A *sulṭān* thus may be described as a proof that is complete and "cuts through" opposition. When Solomon demands that the hoopoe present a *sulṭān* for its absence (27:21), he wants a complete explanation that "cuts off" all objections; such an explanation he does receive (27:22–24). The Idolators (see *idolatry*) are asked to present a *sulṭān* in support of their beliefs (10:68; 18:15).

MANN See CONDESCENSION

MANN AND SALWĀ

Mann was the dew-like substance that dropped on earth for the Israelites during their wanderings in the desert, and constituted, together with *salwā* or quail, the supply of food for them. The provision of *mann* and *salwā* was one of God's special favors to the Israelites (2:57; 7:160; 20:80).

MANSAK See SACRIFICE

MARRIAGE

Arabic: *nikāḥ*

I. General. Islam sanctions, promotes, and protects the institution of marriage. Marriage constitutes the legitimate foundation of the family, and the family is the means of perpetuating the human race (16:72). 30:21 describes the purpose of marriage as *sukūn*, which implies both sexual gratification and mental peace (see also 7:189). According to the same verse, the true foundation of marriage is "love and compassion."

24:32 encourages society to marry off the unmarried, including male and female slaves. A man who cannot marry a freewoman may marry a Muslim female slave (see *slavery*; 4:25).

Having established the institution of marriage on a firm footing, the Qur'ān strictly forbids adultery (*q.v.*). 2:102 condemns those who seek to destroy the institution of marriage by trying to effect separation between husband and wife.

II. Betrothal, Polygyny, Marriage with non-Muslims. Marriage is preceded by betrothal. It is forbidden to make a formal proposal to a widow who is completing her waiting period (*q.v.*; 2:235).

4:3 allows polygyny, limiting to four the maximun number of wives one may have at one time, and further stipulates that one must treat all one's wives justly and equally, otherwise have only one wife (see also 4:129).

2:221 forbids Muslim men and women to marry "idolators" (see *idolatry*). 5:5 allows a Muslim man to marry a female member of the People of the Book (*q.v.*), but a Muslim female may not do so (see *the lawful and the unlawful*), as the prohibition against marrying "disbelieving" and "idolatrous" men (2:221; 60:10) is in this case understood to apply to all non-Muslims.

III. Marriage—More than a Contract. Technically,

marriage is a contract (*^c^uqdat an-nikāḥ* ["knot or bond of marriage"]; 2:235, 237) between two parties. As such, it is not indissoluble. At the same time, marriage is more than a contract, for it involves a serious moral commitment; it is a "strong pact" or "firm covenant" (4:21). Another word used for marriage is *iḥṣān* (4:24, 25; 5:5), the "protection" a man offers to a woman on a permanent basis. This, too, makes marriage more than a contract.

IV. Rights and Obligations of Spouses. The rights of one spouse are the obligations of the other. The spouses have similar rights, though the man, being the head (*qawwām* ["caretaker, manager"]) of the family unit, and being responsible for, among other things, the maintenance of the wife (2:228), has "a degree above" the woman (4:34). The man has the right to expect obedience from his wife (4:34), and, if she is disobedient, may take a series of actions against her (see *nushūz*). He must treat his wife with kindness (4:19). If he has more than one wife, he must treat them fairly (see above). Upon marrying a woman, a man must pay her dower (*q.v.*). And, upon divorcing one's wife, he must make financial compensation for the hurt or damage done by the severance of relations (2:241) and not prevent her from marrying another man (2:232). Generally speaking, the relations between husband and wife should be governed by considerations of love and kindness (30:21), and peace and harmony (4:128). Husband and wife are called "dress" to each other (see *dress*).

See also: ADULTERY; DIVORCE; DOUBLE SWEARING; DOWER; DRESS; FALSE ALLEGATION OF UNCHASTITY; LAWFUL AND THE UNLAWFUL, THE; NUSHŪZ; OATH OF SEXUAL ABSTINENCE.

MARTYRDOM See WITNESS

MA^C^RŪF See CUSTOMARY LAW; ENJOINING GOOD AND FORBIDDING EVIL

MASH^{c}AR AL-ḤARĀM, AL- See SACRED LANDMARK, THE

MASJID AL-AQṢĀ, AL- See DISTANT MOSQUE, THE

MASJID AL-ḤARĀM, AL- See SACRED MOSQUE, THE

MAWQŪDHAH See LAWFUL AND THE UNLAWFUL, THE

MAWT See DEATH

MAYSIR See WINE AND GAME OF CHANCE

MEDIAN COMMUNITY, THE

Arabic: *ummah wasaṭ.*

2:143 calls Muslims the "median community." The explanation usually given of the title is that the religion of Muslims, Islam, avoids the extremes of Judaism and Christianity—the "severities" of Judaism and the "laxities" of Christianity. But, taken in its context, the "median community" may simply be interpreted as the community that sticks to the highway of religion—the "median path" (see *the right path*)—instead of wandering off into byways, that is, becoming involved in factionalism and sectarianism. As such, the title of "median community" is not only a prerogative, but carries with it a responsibility also—the responsibility to stay on the median path and guide others to it.

See also: RIGHT PATH, THE.

MEDIAN PATH, THE See MEDIAN COMMUNITY, THE; RIGHT PATH, THE

MESSENGER See PROPHET

MILK AL-YAMĪN See SLAVERY

MINOR SIN See MAJOR SIN AND MINOR SIN

MIRACLE

I. Reality of Miracles. The Qur'ān speaks of many miracles performed by prophets with the sanction of God or wrought by God through prophets. Abraham was thrown into a fire by a king, but the fire became "cool and safe" for him (21:68–69). Abraham was blessed with a son though his wife was past the age of childbearing (11:72), and Zechariah was similarly blessed (19:5–7). Moses confronted Pharaoh with "nine clear signs" (17:101), that is, miracles. Jesus' life was full of miracles. He was born without a father (19:20–21), spoke eloquently while still in the cradle (19:29–33), performed a variety of miracles (3:49), and was raised to the heavens by God (3:55; 4:158).

These and other incidents related in the Qur'ān leave no doubt that, according to the Qur'ān, miracles are quite possible and have in fact occurred. The basic question the Qur'ān seems to be posing in this connection is, whether God, Who gave the physical universe its laws, has, after establishing those laws, lost the capacity to suspend, alter, or break those laws. In other words, the question of miracles cannot be decided in the abstract, but must be viewed in relation to the power of God. When Abraham's wife wondered how she could give birth at such an advanced age, the angels said, "Are you surprised at the ways of God?" (11:72–73; see also 19:8–9).

II. Miracles and Magic. When Moses performed his miracles before Pharaoh, the latter called him a magician (10:76; 20:63; 26:34). Moses replied (17:102) that his miracles could not have been the result of magic, but were "eye-opening signs" (*baṣā'ir*) which could be shown only with the help of God. According to this verse, a miracle is self-evidently different from a magical feat. That is why Pharaoh's magicians, when they saw Moses turn his staff into a serpent, acknowledged that it was no magical feat and prostrated themselves before God (7:119–122; 20:70; 26:46–48). The fact that they lost no time in making this acknowledgment indicates that a magician, more than anyone else, is in a position to distinguish between magic and a miracle and to testify that the source of a miracle, unlike that of a magical feat, is God and not a human being.

III. When are Miracles Shown? Miracles are shown at the demand of a disbelieving or rebellious people. Skeptical peoples have frequently challenged prophets to perform miracles, though almost always they have persisted in their disbelief even after their demand has been met (17:59), for the demand is prompted not by a genuine desire to see the truth verified, but by complacent wickedness.

IV. Qur'ān as Miracle. Muḥammad's opponents repeatedly asked him to show a miracle to prove that he was a true prophet (6:8; 11:31; 17:90–93; 21:5). The Qur'ān's reply to such demands was that the Qur'ān is enough of a miracle (29:51: "Is it not sufficient for them that We have revealed to you The Book, which is recited to them?")—as are nature and history—and that miracles, which seldom convinced earlier nations, would not convince Muḥammad's opponents (2:99, 118; 6:7, 25, 109; 17:59; 54:2.)

See also: ḤAWĀRĪ; MAGIC.

MISERLINESS

Arabic: *bukhl.*

Miserliness is condemned. What is particularly condemned is miserliness in spending of one's wealth in the way of God. In the hereafter, misers will be punished by means of their own wealth: the gold and silver they hoarded up in the world will be heated in the fire of hell and used to brand their foreheads and sides (9:34–35; also 3:180). The Qur'ān notes the psychology of a miserly person: being miserly himself, he wants others to be like him (4:37; 57:24), so that he is not singled out for being the way he is. A rich but stingy person acts as if he has acquired his wealth by his own effort, whereas in reality all wealth is a gift from God (3:180; 4:37; 9:76).

See also: EXTRAVAGANCE; MODERATION; SPENDING IN THE WAY OF GOD.

MISGUIDANCE

Arabic: *ḍalāl, ḍalālah* ("misguidance"); *iḍlāl* ("to misguide).

According to certain Qur'ānic verses, God misguides whomever He likes, and no one can guide the one whom He has misguided (e.g. 4:88; 7:186; 13:33; 39:23). But such verses do not mean that God guides and misguides arbitrarily. What is meant is that certain people, through constant preoccupation with evil, render themselves unworthy of receiving guidance from God; they "ask for" misguidance, and God misguides them in order to punish them for their sins. When, at Mount Sinai, Moses and the seventy Israelite elders were "shaken up," Moses said to God, "This is but a trial from You, by means of which You misguide whomever You like and guide whomever You like" (7:155). That is to say, God guides those who remain steadfast in trials, proving themselves worthy of being guided, and He misguides those who, after failing the test, prove themselves unworthy of His guidance. 2:26, too, says that God guides or misguides whomever He likes, but clarifies the statement by adding that it is only the wicked whom He misguides (see also 14:27; 40:34, 74).

See also: FREEDOM AND DETERMINISM; GUIDANCE.

MISKĪN See NEEDY, THE

MĪTHĀQ See COVENANT

MĪZĀN

Mīzān (literally, "balance, scales") has the following meanings in the Qur'ān:

1. The principle of balance and symmetry that marks the structure of the universe (55:7).

2. The criterion for distinguishing truth from falsehood and telling right from wrong. The word is used in this sense for the Qur'ān in 42:17 and for previous scriptures in 57:25.

3. The scales that will be set up in the hereafter (*q.v.*) for the purpose of weighing the moral actions of men (7:8, 9; 21:47; 23:102, 103; 101:6, 8).

4. The giving of full measure (6:152; 7:85; 11:84, 85; 55:9).

MODERATION

Arabic: *qaṣd, iqtiṣād.*

The Qur'ān advises moderation in financial and other matters. 17:29 says: "Do not tie your hand around your neck [=do not be stingy], nor stretch it out fully [=do not be extravagant]." Luqmān advises his son: "Be modest of carriage" (31:19). And 17:110 says that, during *ṣalāt* (*q.v.*), the Qur'ān should be recited in a voice that is neither too loud nor too low but is "in between the two."

See also: EXTRAVAGANCE; MISERLINESS.

MONK See MONASTICISM

MONASTICISM

Arabic: *rahbāniyyah.*

57:27 calls monasticism an "innovation" and accuses its innovators of poorly acquitting themselves of the responsibilities associated with it. According to the context of the verse, all prophets propagated and endeavored to establish the religion of God and, if necessary, to fight to that end. Jesus was no exception to the rule, even though he did not get the opportunity to actually fight. Like Jesus, the followers of Jesus were specially blessed by God with kind and gentle hearts. But later Christians saw the loving-kindness of Jesus and his early followers as a justification for establishing a full-fledged system of monasticism, thus committing an excess. The Qur'ān seems to be saying that monasticism came into being as a result of basically good intentions, but that it exceeded its proper limits; those who "invented" it suffered from an imbalance of outlook and gave themselves up to monasticism entirely, to the exclusion of other important obligations. For, 57:27 says, God had charged them not with practicing monasticism but with seeking His pleasure, which goal, the verse is implying, could have been accomplished without establishing a whole system of monasticism.

As for monks (*ruhbān*; sing. *rāhib*), the Qur'ān makes a distinction between them, praising those who humbly serve God and are free from pride and conceit (5:82), and criticizing those who are self-serving and wrongfully appropriate others' property (9:34).

See also: ḤIBR; QISSĪS; RABBĀNĪ.

MONOTHEISM

Arabic: **tawḥīd.*

I. General. *Tawḥīd* ("oneness *or* unicity of God") is the Islamic monotheistic doctrine: There is no deity but God

(2:163, 255; 3:2, 6, 18, 62; 4:87, 171; 5:73; 6:19, 102, 106; 14:52; 16:22, 51; 20:8, 14; 22:34; 23:116; 27:26; 28:70, 88; 37:4). God is absolutely One; He has neither children nor partners (17:111; 23:91; 25:2). *Tawḥid* constitutes one of the three principal doctrines of Islam, the other two being prophecy (*q.v.*) and the hereafter (*q.v.*).

II. Original Creed of Mankind. According to the Qur'ān, *tawḥid* is the original creed of mankind, and one that prophets across the ages have sought to preach and revive (2:133; 16:2; 21:25). Noah called his people to *tawḥīd* (7:59; 23:23), and so did Hūd (7:65; 11:50), Ṣāliḥ (7:73; 11:61), Shu^c^ayb (7:85; 11:84), and Muḥammad (7:158; 9:129; 18:110; 21:108; 41:6).

III. Evidence of Tawḥīd. No one may partake of the deity of God since only God is the Creator, Lord, and Maintainer of the heavens and the earth (27:60–61; 35:3; 40:62; 43:87), has all the power and authority (2:107; 3:26, 189; 5:17, 18, 40, 120; 24:42; 42:49; 57:5; 85:9), has the power to give life and cause death (44:8), listens to the calls of those in distress, delivering them from their trouble (10:22–23; 17:67; 27:62–63), guides men through the "darknesses" of land and sea (6:63, 97; 27:63), and provides them with sustenance (10:31; 27:60; 35:3).

Evidence of *tawḥīd* is to be found not only in external nature, but in man's own being as well; at times of crisis, man forgets all those he has set up as partners to God and calls upon the One God (see *covenant, idolatry*).

IV. Behavioral Dimension. *Tawḥīd* is supposed to have certain behavioral manifestations. For it is not simply belief in God on a doctrinal level, it is also behavior in accordance with the demands of that doctrine. Thus, sovereignty and power belong to God alone (6:57, 62; 12:40, 67), and he who passes judgments in accordance with the law of other than God commits great wrong (5:44, 45, 47). Also, God has caused all human beings to descend from a single pair of human beings (4:1); the oneness of God implies the oneness of humanity and entails responsibilities toward the other members of society. The doctrine of *tawḥīd* is thus the basis of Islamic social humanism.

See also: ALLĀH; DĪN; IDOLATRY.

MOTHER CITY

Arabic: *umm al-qurā.*

Makkah is called the "mother city" (literally, "mother of cities") in 6:92 and 42:7 because, both politically and religiously, it was the hub and omphalos of Arabia. According to the two verses, Muḥammad was raised as prophet "so that he may warn the [people of the] mother city and those around it." The verses imply that prophets are raised in areas which are nerve centers in a land and are crucial from the viewpoint of bringing social change.

See also: SANCTUARY OF PEACE, THE.

MU'ALLAFAT AL-QULŪB See ZAKĀT

MUBASHSHIR See GIVER OF GOOD TIDINGS

MUBĀYAᶜAH See OATH OF ALLEGIANCE

MUHĀJARAH See EMIGRATION

MUḤĀRABAH See FIGHTING AGAINST GOD AND HIS PROPHET

MUHAYMIN See QUR'ĀN

MUḤKAMĀT See QUR'ĀN

MUKĀTABAH See SLAVERY

MUNĀFIQ See HYPOCRITES, THE

MUNDHIR See WARNER

MUNKAR See ENJOINING GOOD AND FORBIDDING EVIL

MUNKHANIQAH See LAWFUL AND THE UNLAWFUL, THE

MUSLIM See DĪN; ISLAM

MUTARADDIYAH See LAWFUL AND THE UNLAWFUL, THE

MUTASHĀBIHĀT See QUR'ĀN

MUTUAL CURSING See DOUBLE SWEARING

N

NABĪ See PROPHET

NADHĪR See WARNER

NADHR See VOW

NAFS AL-AMMĀRAH, AN- See BIDDING SELF, THE

NAFS AL-LAWWĀMAH, AL- See CENSORIOUS SELF, THE

NAFS AL-MUṬMA'INNAH, AL- See CONTENTED SELF, THE

NAJWĀ

Najwā (or *tanājī*) is "confidential talk, private conversation, secret deliberations." While *najwā* may have a positive or neutral connotation (19:52: on Mount Sinai, God spoke with Moses "in confidence"; 12:80: Joseph's brothers, on seeing that Benjamin had been detained by the Egyptian authorities, moved aside in order to discuss the matter privately), the word is often used in the Qur'ān with the negative meaning of "conspiracy." 17:47 warns Muḥammad's opponents, saying that God knows about their *najwā* which is aimed at preparing schemes to thwart Muḥammad (see also 4:114; 9:78; 21:3; 43:80). When Moses rebuked Pharaoh, Pharaoh and his courtiers held *najwā* in order to devise a cunning scheme against Moses (20:62).

Najwā is one of the main themes of S. 58. The sūrah criticizes the Hypocrites (*q.v.*) for starting a whispering campaign among the Muslims in order to vilify Islam and discredit the Prophet. Vs. 7 warns them that God is aware of their secret conferences; vs. 8 lays bare the evil objectives of their *najwā*; and vs. 9, addressing the Muslims, says that their own *najwā* should be to promote good; vs. 10, again speaking of the Hypocrites, says that their *najwā* is inspired by Satan (*q.v.*). Vs. 12 of the sūrah enjoins the giving of *ṣadaqah* (*q.v.*) before holding *najwā* with the Prophet. The injunction was aimed at preventing the Hypocrites from wasting the Prophet's time; eager to remain in the good graces of the Prophet and malign others in his eyes, the Hypocrites often sought private audience with him. Vs. 13 repeals the injunction of paying the *ṣadaqah*, presumably because the objective envisaged in vs. 12 had been achieved.

NASĪ' See INTERCALATION

NASKH See ABROGATION

NAṬĪḤAH See LAWFUL AND THE UNLAWFUL, THE

NATURE

Two main points are made about nature. First, nature (or the universe, with everything it contains—"whatever is in the heavens and in the earth" [31:20; 45:13]) has been "subjugated" (*taskhīr*) for man (14:32; 16:12, 14; 22:65; 31:20; 45:12-). That is to say, man has been given the power and ability to study it, discover its laws, and control it, thus harnessing it for his use and benefit. Second, nature with all its plenitude constitutes a "sign" (*āyah* [*q.v.*]), or rather a multitude of signs (2:164; 3:190; 10:5–6; 12:105; 13:3–4; 16:79; 36:33–42; 45:3–5; 78:6–16; 80:24–32). That is, it points toward God. The two points are obviously connected: subjugation of nature for man constitutes a great bounty of which God has made man the recipient, and it falls to man to recognize that and be grateful to Him, nature itself thus pointing to the source of the bounty.

NATURE, HUMAN See FIṬRAH

NECESSITY

Arabic: *iḍṭirār*.

2:173 allows the eating of forbidden food, but lays down two conditions. First, in eating that food, one must have no intention of breaking the law, that is, one must remember that one is doing so out of necessity and not be secretly pleased at the opportunity of laying one's hands on the forbidden food. Second, one must eat only the amount necessary to save one's life or avert the emergency. The order in which the two conditions are stated—no intention of breaking the law, and eating only the necessary amount—is significant: even in a situation of emergency, the Qur'ān's primary concern is maintaining the right ethical perspective on actions (see also 5:3).

See also: COMPULSION; DISSIMULATION.

NEEDY, THE

Several words are used:

1. *Faqīr.* A *faqīr* (pl. *fuqarā'*) is one who is poor. The word is an antonym of *ghanī* ("rich"), and so any person who lacks resources and is consequently in need is a *faqīr*, irrespective of whether he begs for help or not (cf. *sā'il*, below). *Fuqarā'* are entitled to a share in *ṣadaqāt* (see *ṣadaqah*; 2:271), including *zakāt* (*q.v.*; 9:60), and in the spoils (*q.v.*).

2. *Miskīn.* A *miskīn* (pl. *masākīn*) is one who, in addition to being a *faqīr*, also lacks the ability or means to make an effort to earn his living. *Masākīn* may be supported out of the *zakāt* fund, and also out of the spoils.

3. *Sā'il.* A *sā'il* (pl. *sā'ilūn*) is one who begs for help. The Qur'ān seems to suggest that if a person begs for help, then one should help him if possible, and not make detailed inquiries as to whether he really needs assistance (2:177; 51:19; 70:25; cf. *faqīr,* above); if one cannot help him, one should at least not rebuke him (93:10).

4. *Maḥrūm.* A *maḥrūm* (pl. *maḥrūmūn*), as the word suggests, is one who was at one time fortunately situated, but was subsequently "deprived" of his wealth as a result of, for example, a business setback. One who is *maḥrūm* has a right to financial help from those who are well off (51:19; 70:25).

See also: ORPHAN.

NEIGHBOR

Neighbors are of two kinds—relative (*al-jār dhū l-qurbā*) and non-relative (*al-jār al-junub*). Both ought to be treated kindly (4:36).

NIGHT OF DECREE, THE

Arabic: *laylat al-qadr.*

I. Name and Identification. According to 97:1, the Qur'ān was revealed on the Night of Decree (literally, "Determining"). 44:3 says that the Qur'ān was revealed on a "blessed night," and the next verse describes this night as the one during. which important matters are decided 2:185 says that the Qur'ān was revealed in Ramaḍān (*q.v.*). From these verses it can be gathered that the Night of Decree falls in Ramaḍān (according to some *aḥādīth*, in the last ten days of Ramaḍān), and that it is an important night in the divine calendar since important decisions regarding the world and its administration are reached in it. Since 44:4 uses the word *yufraqu*, suggesting that matters are "decided" (literally, "distinguished") during that night, the word *qadr* in 97:1 should perhaps be translated "decree." Incidentally, the statements that the Qur'ān was revealed on a certain night do not necessarily mean that the whole of it was revealed on that night; according to 17:106 (see also 25:32) the Qur'ān was revealed in portions over a long period of time. The statements therefore need only signify that the decision to reveal the Qur'ān was made on that night, and that the first revelation was given on that night (see *Qur'ān*).

II. Significance of the Night. In view of the above, 97:1 would signify that the revelation of the Qur'ān is a momentous matter, and that the Qur'ān is not to be taken lightly since it is part of the overall divine scheme. During the Night of Decree, Gabriel and other angels descend to the earth in order to carry out the commandments of God (97:4). Furthermore, the night guarantees complete peace and security that lasts until dawn (97:5), which implies that satans (see *Satan*) are placed under a heavenly curfew until daybreak. One implication of this verse in the larger Qur'ānic context is that the Qur'ān is not to be confused with the discourse of a poet or a soothsayer, for soothsayers and poets present their discourse with the aid and abetment of evil *jinn* (*q.v.*), but since the satanic host—including the evil *jinn*—are on that night placed under a heavenly curfew, they could not have interfered with the revelation that Gabriel brought from the heavens in that night.

Being an important night in the divine calendar, the Night of Decree carries with it great blessings. For those who may seek its blessings (through worship and remembrance of God), this night is "better than a thousand years" (97:3), an expression that may be taken literally but may also be interpreted to mean numberless blessings.

NIKĀḤ See MARRIAGE

NULLIFICATION OF DEEDS

Arabic: *ḥabṭ al-aᶜmāl.*

The word "deeds" in the phrase means "good deeds," and the phrase signifies that, just as good actions wipe off bad actions (11:114), so bad actions set good actions at naught and will fetch no reward in the hereafter. Good actions which are performed, for instance, in a state of disbelief (*q.v.*), idolatry (*q.v.*), or apostasy (*q.v.*), or in defiance of God and His commandments will bear no fruit in the hereafter (2:217; 6:88; 9:17; 18:104–105; 33:19; 39:65; 47:8–9, 32; see also 3:21–22; 7:147). Similarly, those who live for this world and have no thought for the next world will find that any good actions they might have performed in this world are of no use to them in the next (11:16). In certain cases, good deeds may prove to be unfruitful even when performed in a state of belief. A Muslim who kills another Muslim on purpose will lose all his reward in the hereafter (4:93), as will a believer who conducts himself like a disbeliever (5:5). 49:2 warns Muslims to desist from showing disrespect to the Prophet, otherwise their actions will bear no fruit.

NUSHŪZ

Literally, *nushūz* means "to rise up." Technically, it may be rendered as "intransigence" of a spouse. Depending on which spouse commits it, the intransigence may take a different form.

I. Nushūz as Disobedience by Wife. The wife's *nushūz* takes the form of "rebellion." The wife, that is to say, challenges the husband's authority and openly defies him. The Qur'ān considers this a very serious matter, and 4:34 allows the husband to take three measures: (a) advice and instruction; (b) denial of conjugal rights; (c) physical chastisement. The three must be taken in that order, the second failing the first, the third failing the second. Also, "physical chastisement" must not be confused with "wife battering," something that is disallowed by the spirit of the Qur'ān and forbidden by clear statements in *Ḥadīth*. Indeed, Muslim jurists stipulate that a toothstick be used to strike the wife.

II. Nushūz as Indifference by Husband. The *nushūz* of the husband takes the form of indifference. The relevant text here is 4:128. The pithy verse may be explained as follows: If a wife senses that her husband is apathetic toward her or has lost interest in her (e.g. because of her sterility or chroninc illness), she should, in the interest of saving the marriage, try to reach a compromise with him by relieving him of some of the obligations he is supposed to discharge toward her. At the same time, the verse appeals to the husband to be large-hearted and treat his wife justly and kindly regardless of how he feels towards her.

See also: MARRIAGE.

NUṢUB See LAWFUL AND THE UNLAWFUL, THE

NUSUK See SACRIFICE

O

OATH

Arabic: *ḥalf* or *ḥilf*; *qasam* (pl. *aqsām*); *yamīn* (pl. *aymān*).

I. General. Barring oaths that are sworn thoughtlessly and are neither meant nor taken seriously (2:225; 5:89), one should feel responsible for the oath one has sworn; one must "guard" one's oath (5:89), i.e. try one's utmost to fullfil it (16:91; also 4:33), and, in case one breaks it, make atonement (*q.v.*) for it (5:89; 66:2). One must not use the name of God in swearing an oath to do something improper or unlawful (2:224; 16:92, 94; see *atonement*).

II. Legal Value. In certain situations an oath may have legal implications. One such situation is described in 5:106–108. If death approaches one at the time of making a will (see *bequest*), one should have two "just" persons serve as witnesses, and the witnesses should swear a solemn oath that they shall report the truth; two non-Muslims may be taken as witnesses if Muslim witnesses are not available, as might happen during travel. If it is later discovered that the witnesses have sought to wrong one of the heirs by misrepresenting the terms of the will, two persons from the wronged party may make a rejoinder on oath, in which case the testimony of the original witnesses will be invalidated. This check is supposed to induce the original witnesses to bear true witness.

The word *yamīn* in 9:12–13 is to be understood in the sense of political "commitment" or "pact." The verses refer to the pact between Muslims and pagan Arabs. According to them, the breaking of such an agreement by one party entitles the other to take action against it.

III. Oath as Pretense. The Qur'ān criticizes the Hypocrites (*q.v.*) for swearing oaths by God in order to shield themselves from criticism and hide their nefarious aims (58:16; 63:2), and to convince the Prophet and the Muslims that they were on their side (5:53) and, if called upon to do so, would support them in battle (24:53).

The Qur'ān also criticizes the Makkans, who, before Muḥammad was raised as prophet, had sworn that if a prophet were to arise among them, they would prove to be better believers than the People of the Book (*q.v.*; 35:42), but who, after Muḥammad had announced his prophecy, began to ask for miracles (see *miracle*), saying that they would definitely believe if they were shown one (6:109).

See also: ATONEMENT; DIVORCE; OATH OF ALLEGIANCE; OATH OF SEXUAL ABSTINENCE; OATH-MONGER.

OATH OF ALLEGIANCE

Arabic: **bay^{c}ah, mubāya^{c}ah.*

In a critical situation the ruler of the Muslim community may take an oath of allegiance from the members of the community as a sign of their commitment to a certain cause. When Muḥammad made the Pact of Ḥudaybiyyah with the Makkans (628), the report that the Makkans were holding Muḥammad's envoy hostage created a very critical situation, and Muḥammad had the Muslims accompanying him pledge that they would not hesitate to lay down their lives if the occasion called for it. The Qur'ān praises those who took the oath of allegiance on that occasion (48:18).

OATH OF SEXUAL ABSTINENCE

Arabic: *īlā'*.

Īlā' is the oath of sexual abstinence taken by the husband. 2:226 lays down four months as the maximum allowable period for *īlā'*, after which the husband must either divorce his wife or break the oath.

See also: DIVORCE.

OATHMONGER

Arabic: *ḥallāf*.

68:10 advises Muḥammad not to listen to those who swear oaths indiscriminately. The reference is to Quraysh leaders, who, unable to make a cogent case against the Prophet, swore to their followers that Muḥammad was either a poet, a sorcerer (see *magic*), or a man possessed.

By using the word *mahīn* ("base, mean") along with *ḥallāf*, the verse explains the psychology of the people who swear oaths indiscriminately: being acutely conscious of the falsity of their claims, they swear oaths in order to fortify their claims against doubt or criticism. Lacking self-respect, they do not think their word will be taken at face value, and so they swear oaths in order to establish their credit.

ORIGINAL SIN, THE See FORGIVENESS; MAN; REPENTANCE

ORPHAN

Arabic: *yatīm* (pl. *yatāmā*).

A Muslim community is responsible fot taking care of its orphans. The Qur'ān criticizes the affluent Quraysh of Makkah for neglecting society's needy members (see *the needy*), among them orphans (89:17). On several occasions the Qur'ān mentions orphans along with parents and relatives as those who deserve kind treatment (2:83, 215; 4:36). Orphans have a share in the community's wealth (2:177, 215; see also *spoils*). One of the marks of an Islamic community is that, in it, an orphan not only gets food, clothing, and shelter, he also enjoys respect (89:17). That is to say, not only does no stigma attach to him, he has a position of honor in society. According to 93:6, one of the blessings of God on Muḥammad was that He found him an orphan and gave him refuge. The verse, incidentally, is another critique of the Makkan social set-up.

See also: NEEDY, THE.

OSTENTATION

Arabic: *tabarruj*.

The Arabic word comes from *burj*, which means "minaret." *Tabarruj* thus means "to make oneself conspicuous like a minaret." In Qur'ānic usage, *tabarruj* denotes decking oneself out in order to attract attention. Muslim women are instructed to avoid *tabarruj*, which is associated with the age of ignorance (*q.v.*; 33:33; see also 24:60).

See also: AGE OF IGNORANCE, THE.

P

PARADISE See HEAVEN

PEOPLE OF THE BOOK, THE

Arabic: *ahl al-kitāb.*

I. Meaning. "The People of the Book" are Jews and Christians. The "Book" is the Torah, which was *the* Book (*q.v.*) for Christians as well as for Jews. The phrase, while often used of Jews and Christians both (as in 3:65), is sometimes used specifically of Jews (3:72; 4:153) or Christians (3:64; 4:171). The People of the Book are invited to believe in Muḥammad and the Qur'ān (3:110; 5:65); they are told that the Qur'ān is an "objectification" (*taṣdīq*; see *Qur'ān*) of the promises made in their scriptures with regard to the prophecy of Muḥammad (2:41, 89, 91, 97, 101; 3:3, 81; 4:47; 5:46, 48; 6:92; 35:31; 46:30; 61:6). They are asked to judge in accordance with the Torah and the Evangel (5:47, 68), which is usually interpreted by Muslim scholars to mean that the People of the Book should believe in the Qur'ān since their scriptures point to the Qur'ān (see 2:121, 144, 146).

II. Criticism of the People of the Book. The Qur'ān contains some sharp criticism of the People of the Book. They are represented as being envious of Muslims, who had received divine revelation (2:105). They are accused of disbelieving in Muḥammad and the Qur'ān (3:98), of concealing parts of their scriptures (see *distortion of scripture*), of "mixing" truth with falsehood (3:71), of holding extreme and untenable religious views (4:171; 5:77), of believing only selectively in their scriptures (2:85), of confining salvation to followers of Judaism or Christianity (2:113) only, and of attempting to prevent people from converting to Islam or reconvert people to disbelief (2:109; 3:72, 99).

III. Two Types. While the Qur'ān criticizes the People of the Book for their conduct, it does not contain a blanket denunciation of them. Rather, it carefully distinguishes between those of them who are God-fearing, pious, and kindhearted (3:113) and those who are not. That is why it sometimes says that a "certain group" from among them wishes to mislead Muslims (3:69), or that only some, and not all, of the People of the Book use double standards while dealing with those who do not belong to their ranks (3:75; see also 3:100). The Qur'ān also instructs Muslims to argue with the People of the Book in a manner that is good (29:46), and, as is clear from 3:64, wants Muslims to reach a meeting ground with them in order to discuss with them issues of common interest.

IV. Special Status. Furthermore, the Qurān accords the People of the Book a special status, making a distinction between them and the Idolators (see *idolatry*). Unlike the Idolators of Makkah, who were given only two options, those of accepting Islam or facing the sword, the People of the Book were given the option of *jizyah* ("poll-tax"; 9:29). Muslims are allowed to eat the food of the People of the Book, and Muslim men are allowed to marry Jewish and Christian women (see *the lawful and the unlawful; marriage*). The special status is explained by the fact that, in the eyes of the Qur'ān, the People of the Book are, essentially, followers of a revealed religion and believers in the scriptures given by God. Instead of totally rejecting what they stand for, the Qur'ān seeks to "correct" their beliefs and practices.

PERSECUTION See FITNAH

PERSEVERANCE

Arabic: *ṣabr.*

Ṣabr is "persistence, endurance, perseverance." As a Qur'ānic term possessing religious value, it means: to persevere in a good act with a view to achieving the pleasure of God (13:22), and to do so with belief and trust in God (16:42; 29:59).

Ṣabr is an "act of constancy" (3:186; 31:17; 42:43; also 46:35; it typically involves facing danger or loss with resolution, as when life is threatened in battle or some other loss is imminent (2:155, 177), or when one is persecuted by the enemy (14:12). The Israelites were blessed by God on account of their *ṣabr* against their Egyptian oppressors (7:137). Job is praised as *ṣābir* (active participle from *ṣabr*). Jacob is cited for his "excellent" *ṣabr* (12:18, 83), and Muḥammad is instructed to practice similar *ṣabr* (70:5).

But while *ṣabr* is most conspicuously displayed in times of hardship, it is not simply resolution shown in difficult circumstances. 11:10–11 imply that *ṣabr* is also the name for the composed and dignified attitude one adopts in easy and favorable circumstances.

The Qur'ān presents *ṣabr* as a social virtue, that is, as a virtue that the members of the Muslim community should cultivate and help one another cultivate: "O those who have believed, practice *ṣabr* yourselves and [also] help one another practice it" (3:200; also 90:17; 103:3).

PHENOMENAL AND NON-PHENOMENAL REALMS, THE

Arabic: *shahādah* ("phenomenal realm"); *ghayb* ("non-phenomenal realm").

As a technical term, *ghayb* does not simply mean "the

unseen," but all those things which man, with his earthly limitations, has no means of gaining access to, unless, that is, God were to give him access to them. Perhaps a more adequate equivalent would be "the non-perceptible." *Ghayb* in this sense is the opposite of *shahādah*, which would then be the "phenomenal *or* perceptible realm."

God has, and He alone has, complete knowledge of the phenomenal and non-phenomenal worlds (2:33; also 5:109, 116; 6:59; 9:78; 10:20; 11:123; 16:77; 18:26; 27:65; 34:3, 48; 35:38; 49:18). Man has no knowledge of the *ghayb* (6:50; 7:188; 11:31; 27:65; 52:41; 53:35; 68:47), though God may choose to reveal a part of the *ghayb* to prophets (72:26–27).

In Arabian mythology, the *jinn* (*q.v.*) were believed to know the *ghayb*, and contact with them was supposed to give a soothsayer his power of clairvoyance and future-telling. This idea is refuted in the Qur'ān. According to 34:14, the *jinn* who served Solomon were deceived by Solomon's death. Solomon was supervising the work of the *jinn*, and he stood leaning on his staff. It was only when his staff, eaten away by worms, collapsed, causing Solomon to fall, that the *jinn* realized that he had been dead for some time. Had they possessed knowledge of the *ghayb* in any degree, the verse argues, they would not have continued to suffer the humiliation of laboring for Solomon after the latter's death. (See also 72:8–9.)

For "belief in the *ghayb*," see *faith*.

See also: FAITH; WITNESS.

PIETY

Arabic: *birr; taqwā*.

I. Birr. "Piety," the usual translation of *birr*, does not fully convey the spirit of the word. The verb *barra* means "to be true, loyal, dutiful," and is used in expressions meaning "to fulfill one's oath" and "to be dutiful and kind to one's parents." In 2:44 *birr* gives the sense of faithfully carrying out the commandments of religion, and in 2:177, 189 it stands for true and genuine belief as opposed to empty ritualism and spiritless formalism.

II. Taqwā. *Taqwā* literally means "wariness, restraint." As a technical term, it is often translated "piety, righteousness," but perhaps a better translation would be "God-mindedness" or "God-consciousness."

Such examples of *taqwā* as keeping from evil actions (40:9) and curbing one's greed (59:9; 64:16) might suggest that *taqwā* is a negative virtue. In a sense this is true, and it is because this is true that the Qur'ān often mentions *taqwā* together with a complementary positive virtue; it speaks, for example, of "those who have *taqwā* and do good deeds" (7:35; also 4:128, 129; 5:93; 16:128). But even though *taqwā* has a negative character, its importance in the formation of character cannot be overemphasized. Since it is the foundation of good character, the Qur'ān frequently gives it a more comprehensive signification, making it the sole requisite of salvation (*q.v.*; 2:212; 3:15, 198; 4:77; 6:32; 12:109; 13:35; 39:20, 73).

PILGRIMAGE

Arabic: *ḥajj*; *ᶜumrah*.

I. Ḥajj.

1. *General.* Pilgrimage to the Kaᶜabah in certain specific days of the year—in Dhū l-Ḥijjah, the last month of the lunar calendar—is called *ḥajj*. Every adult Muslim must perform it at least once in his lifetime provided he is physically able, and has the financial means, to do so; it is the "right" of God upon men (3:97). The Qur'ān presents the *ḥajj* as a practice dating from the time of Abraham, though it claims to have revived it in its original form after the corruption of its form at the hands of the idolatrous Arabs.

2. *Rites and Etiquette.* A pilgrim performs the *ḥajj* in a state of *iḥrām*, that is, in a state in which one keeps away from certain things as if they were "forbidden"; the outward sign of *iḥrām* is a pair of unstitched white sheets of cloth worn by the pilgrim. During the state of *iḥrām* and *ḥajj* one may not hunt animals (5:1, 95), argue or fight with others, engage in any talk with sexual content, or commit any act of wickedness (2:197). Besides the circumambulation of the Ka^{c}bah and the swift-paced walk between the hills of Ṣafā and Marwah, the *ḥajj* involves a trip from Makkah to the plain of ^{c}Arafāt (east of Makkah) and back, with a stopover, on the way back, first at Muzdalifah (see *the sacred landmark*) and then at Minā, where on 10 Dhū l-Ḥijjah animal sacrifice is made. After the sacrifice the head may be shaved (see *atonement*).

II. ^{c}Umrah.

1. *General.* Pilgrimage to the Ka^{c}bah, if performed at any time of the year excepting the designated *ḥajj* days, is called *^{c}umrah*, usually translated "the lesser pilgrimage." The main difference between the *ḥajj* and the *^{c}umrah* is that, unlike the former, the latter does not involve making a trip to the plain of ^{c}Arafāt. Performance of the *^{c}umrah* is not obligatory, though it is highly recommended.

2. *Relationship with the Ḥajj.* The fact that the Qur'ān mentions the *^{c}umrah* together with the *ḥajj* indicates that the two are closely related. The *^{c}umrah* has been called a rehearsal for the *ḥajj*. Etymologically, *^{c}umrah* means "to flourish, be populous," which signifies that the purpose of the *^{c}umrah* is to make sure that the Ka^{c}bah, the "House of God," thrives and flourishes as a result of visits by pilgrims not only during the *ḥajj* season but in other parts of the year as well.

III. Comparison of Ḥajj and ^{c}Umrah with the Pre-Islamic Pilgrimages. After Abraham not only the rites but also the essential purpose of the *ḥajj* was forgotten, and the *ḥajj* was reduced to an empty, meaningless ritual; instead of being an act of sincere worship, it became a cultural and commercial fair. The Qur'ān seeks to purge the *ḥajj* of such accretions. 2:197 says that *taqwā* (see *piety*) is the best provision a *ḥajj* pilgrim can take along. 2:199, criticizing the exemptions claimed by certain tribes from some of the *ḥajj* rites, says that the rites must be performed by all without distinction.

Pagan Arabs considered it a great sin to perform *ḥajj* and *ᶜumrah* in the same trip. But since this was a great inconvenience to foreign (i.e. non-Makkan) pilgrims, 2:196 exempts such pilgrims from undertaking two separate journeys, one each for *ḥajj* and *ᶜumrah*, and permits them to perform the *ᶜumrah*, put off *iḥrām*, and then perform the *ḥajj*, though in this case animal sacrifice must be made, and, if animals are not available, a certain number of fasts observed (see *atonement*).

2:196 enjoins that *ḥajj* and *ᶜumrah* be performed for the sake of God only. The verse implies that the two pilgrimages, while they were performed before Islam, were not performed *for the sake of God*. During the pilgrimages, homage was paid to many other deities besides God. And, as noted above, the pilgrimages had practically lost their religious character.

See also: KAᶜBAH; SACRED LANDMARK, THE; SACRED MOSQUE, THE.

POLYGYNY See MARRIAGE

POLYTHEISM See IDOLATRY

PRAYER

Arabic: *duᶜā'*.

The Qur'ān criticizes the idolatrous Arabs (see *idolatry*) for their practice of calling upon deities other than Allāh. Since God is the only deity, and since He alone has the power to benefit or harm men, one must pray only to

Him for help (6:71; 10:106; 22:12). Beings other than God who are called upon by man are, like man, creatures of God and are powerless to help him (7:194, 197; 16:20; 17:56; 39:38; 40:20; also 22:73; 35:13, 40). At a time of crisis, man calls upon God, forgetting all other deities (17:67), a fact that is made in the Qur'ān the basis of the argument that in the inmost recesses of his being man recognizes only One God (6:63; see *covenant; fiṭrah*).

Under all circumstances, therefore, one must turn only to God for help. God alone listens to prayers (3:38; 27:62; 40:60), and He listens not from afar but from close quarters (2:186). Unfortunately, man's most earnest prayers to God are usually made in times of distress or hardship. If God were to relieve me of my present difficulty, man usually says, I shall live the rest of my life in obedience to Him. But as soon as God relieves him of the difficulty, man becomes forgetful of Him (6:40–41; 7:189–190; 10:12; 29:65; 30:33; 31:32; 39:8; 41:51).

The best way to pray is with humility and in seclusion (7:55). The best time for prayer is the middle of the night, when one abandons one's sleep and calls upon God "in hope [of reward] and out of fear [of punishment]" (32:16).

See also: ṢALĀT.

PRAYER, RITUAL See ṢALĀT

PREDESTINATION See FREEDOM AND DETERMINISM

PRESCRIPTIONS OF GOD

Arabic: *ḥudūd Allāh.*

The "prescriptions of God" are the commandments of God. The word *ḥudūd* literally means "boundaries, limits." Not only must one desist from overstepping the boundaries or limits set by God (2:229), one must stay quite clear of them: "These are the boundaries of God, so do not [even] approach them" (2:187). Although a number of Qur'ānic verses identify particular regulations or instructions as "prescriptions of God" (2:187, 229-230; 4:13–14; 58:4; 65:1), the expression is a general one and includes all kinds of commandments given in the Quran, the more general meaning being indicated by 9:97, 112.

PRESERVED TABLET, THE

Arabic: *lawḥ maḥfūẓ*.

According to 85:22, the Qur'ān is contained in a "Preserved Tablet." One of the charges brought by the Makkans against Muḥammad was that, like poets and soothsayers, he received inspiration from the *jinn* (*q.v.*) but passed it off as divine revelation. The statement that the source of the Qur'ān is the Preserved Tablet means that the Tablet is protected against the encroachments of evil *jinn*; in other words, what Muḥammad receives is divine revelation in its pure form, and angels (see *angel*), not *jinn*, are the medium through which it reaches him.

See also: UMM AL-KITĀB.

PRIDE

Arabic: *takabbur, istikbār*.

I. Pride as Sin. The Qur'ān regards pride as a great sin and condemns it. Pride often leads to the denial of truth. 16:22 says: "As for those who do not believe in the hereafter, their hearts deny, and they are suffering from pride." The last part of the verse, "and they are suffering from pride," states the cause of what precedes immediately, "their hearts deny" (see also 39:59). It was out of pride that Satan (*q.v.*) refused to bow to Adam (2:34; 7:13; 38:74–76), and it was pride that prevented Pharaoh from recognizing Moses as prophet (10:75; 23:45–46; 28:39).

II. Causes of Pride. The following are some of the causes of pride:

1. *Affluence.* Affluent peoples have often rejected prophets because, smug in their affluence, they have refused to recognize the need for any divine guidance. The Quraysh are a case in point (see 96:6–7).

2. *Sense of Superiority.* Satan refused to bow to Adam because he thought he was made of fire which is superior to earth, of which Adam was made (7:12; 38:75–76).

3. *Whims and Desires.* The Israelites repudiated many of God's messengers because the latter brought with them injunctions that went against the former's whims and desires (2:87).

The principal cause of pride, of course, is an exaggerated sense of self-importance.

III. Punishment of Pride. God does not like those who are prideful (16:23). Those who, in their pride, disbelieve in God and reject His prophets and the message brought by them are deprived of the capacity to appreciate the signs of God and receive guidance (7:146; 40:35; see *sealing*). Many nations were destroyed by God because of their overweening pride (41:15–16). In the next world, pride will be punished with hellfire (7:36; 39:60, 72; 46:20).

PROOF, MANIFEST See MANIFEST PROOF

PROPHECY

Arabic: *nubuwwah*; *risālah.*

I. General. The Qur'ān regards the institution of prophecy as a necessary one. There are certain truths that are essential to a wholesome moral and social life on earth, but man, with the limitations under which he naturally labors, lacks access to them. God has, therefore, taken it upon Himself to convey those truths to man, and prophecy is the medium through which He does so.

Belief in prophecy is one of the three main foundations of Islam, the other two being belief in the oneness of God (see *monotheism*) and belief in the hereafter (*q.v.*).

II. History of Prophecy. The Qur'ān does not narrate a complete history of prophecy, saying that it has spoken of some prophets but not all (40:78). Still, it is possible to offer, on the basis of Qur'ānic data, a brief outline of the history of prophecy.

Adam, the first man, was also the first prophet. The next major prophet was Noah, who lived for 950 years (29:14). But it was Abraham who became the ancestor of the most famous line of prophets, which included Ishmael, Isaac, Jacob, Joseph, David, and Solomon. Among the most important prophets are Moses and Jesus. Muḥammad was sent as a prophet for the whole mankind (7:158; 34:28), and he is the final prophet (see *the seal of the prophets*).

Different prophets possessed different types of distinctions; the distinction of Moses, for example, was that God spoke with him (2:253; 4:164). But this should not lead one to believe in some prophets and reject others, for all prophets brought the same essential message, namely, that mankind should worship God alone (16:36; 21:25; 23:32). This is the basis of the Islamic notion that the institution of prophecy is indivisible and that one must believe in all prophets (see *discrimination between prophets*).

See also: DISCRIMINATION BETWEEN PROPHETS; PROPHET; REVELATION; SEAL OF THE PROPHETS, THE.

PROPHET

Arabic: *nabī*; *rasūl*.

I. General. A prophet is one who brings a message from God to a people. Prophets are appointed by God (3:179; 6:124; 22:75). God has raised one or more prophets among every people (10:47; 16:36). Muḥammad, the last prophet (see *the seal of the prophets*), is described as a prophet sent to all mankind (7:158; 34:28).

II. Position and Functions of a Prophet. A prophet, since he is appointed by God, holds a special place in his community. He enjoys a position of authority, given to him by God (4:64), and his commands are to be obeyed just as are the commands of God which he conveys to his people (3:32, 132; 4:59; 5:92; 8:1, 20, 46; 24:56; 47:33; 59:7; 64:12). In every matter pertaining to religion, his verdict is final and must be ungrudgingly accepted by all believers (33:36). Obeying the prophet is practically the same as obeying God Himself (4:80). Obedience to the prophet is one of the conditions of salvation (*q.v.*) in the hereafter (*q.v.*), and disobedience to him results in damnation (4:13–14; 9:63; 24:52; 33:71; 48:13, 17; 72:23). In addition to believing in God, therefore, one must believe in prophets as well (4:136; 24:62; 49:15).

A prophet not only brings a message from God to his people, he also lives out that message in practice; he is the embodiment of that message, which cannot be fully understood without reference to his life. It is for this reason that the life of Muḥammad is called "exemplary conduct" (*uswah ḥasanah*; 33:21).

A prophet gives his people the good tidings that they shall achieve salvation upon accepting his message (see *giver of good tidings*); at the same time he warns them of the consequences of rejecting his message (see *warner*).

It is not the duty of a prophet to forcefully convert people. He is only responsible for communicating the message from God (5:92, 99; 16:35; 24:54; 29:18; 42:48; 64:12), so that, in the hereafter, no nation may present the excuse that it did not receive a message from God (4:165). In the hereafter, prophets will testify that they faithfully conveyed the message of God to their nations (2:143; 4:41; 16:89).

III. Distinction between Nabī and Rasūl. That the

Qur'ān makes a distinction between a *nabī* ("prophet") and a *rasūl* ("messenger") is clear from 22:52, which says that God has never sent "a *rasūl* or a *nabī*" but that Satan has tried to thwart him in his mission. According to Iṣlāḥī, a *rasūl* is different from a *nabī* in that, unlike the latter, he cannot be defied with impunity; unlike a *nabī*, a *rasūl* presents his people with a final warning, after which that people, if it persists in disbelief, is necessarily overtaken by punishment *in this world*. A *nabī* may warn his people of punishment in the next world, but a *rasūl* warns his people of terrestrial punishment as well. Thus every *rasūl* is a *nabī*, but not every *nabī* is a *rasūl*. Verses like 10:47; 13:34; and 58:21 lend support to Iṣlāḥī's view. Strictly speaking, the two words should be translated differently (*nabī* = prophet, *rasūl* = messenger), though in most contexts, for convenience' sake, "prophet" may be used as a translation for both, as it has been in the present work.

IV. Prophets among the Jinn. According to the Qur'ān, the *jinn* (*q.v.*) have had their own prophets. Speaking of the prophets raised among mankind, the Qur'ān frequently emphasizes that they were human beings (14:10–11; 11:27; 16:43, 103; 17:94; 18:110; 21:3, 7; 23:24, 33–34, 47; 26:154, 186; 36:15; 41:6; 54:24; 64:6), implying clearly that only humans could have served as prophets for humans. It also says that every prophet spoke the language of his people (14:4). Furthermore, 17:95 says, replying to the demand that an angel should have been sent as prophet, that if the earth had been peopled by angels, God would have raised angels as prophets in their midst. From all this it is a logical inference to draw that only *jinn* prophets could have been raised to guide the *jinn*. The inference finds explicit support in 6:130, which states that both humans and *jinn* have had prophets raised from among themselves. It is, therefore, incorrect to think that Muḥammad, or any other (human) prophet, prophesied to the *jinn* as well. The verses that are usually cited to prove that Muḥammad prophesied to the *jinn* (46:29–32; 72:1–15) in fact prove the contrary.

See also: DISCRIMINATION BETWEEN PROPHETS; GIVER OF GOOD TIDINGS; PROPHECY; REVELATION; WARNER.

PROSTITUTION See COMPULSION

PROVIDENCE See RABB

PUNISHMENT

Arabic: *ᶜadhāb.*

I. Punishment for Disbelief. Disbelief in the verities of religion entails punishment in the next world, though punishment in this world necessarily results from rejection of a *rasūl* (see *prophet*).

Punishment in this world may be dealt in several ways. For example, the people of Noah were destroyed by means of a flood (10:73; 11:44); Pharaoh and his troops were drowned in the sea (2:50; 8:54; 20:78), and, later on, Egypt fell into economic ruin (7:137); the ᶜĀd were overtaken by a fierce storm—"a barren wind" (51:41) that "for seven nights and eight days" wreaked havoc upon them (69:6–7); and the Thamūd were destroyed by thunder (7:78; 51:44). The punishment, though it comes after many warnings and has an appointed time, comes all of a sudden when it does, giving the guilty people no opportunity to repent (6:44, 47; 7:95; 12:107; 29:53; 42:14).

Punishment in the next world will take the form of hellfire (see *hell*). Unlike the reward for good actions, which will be given manifold (see *reward*), the punishment for evil actions will be proportionate to the evil perpetrated (6:160; 28:84).

II. Punishment for Crimes. The crimes for which punishment is prescribed in the Qur'ān include adultery (*q.v.*), false allegation of unchastity (*q.v.*), fighting against God and His prophet (*q.v.*), murder (see *qiṣās*), and theft (*q.v.*).

See also: ACCOUNTABILITY; RECOMPENSE; RESPITE; REWARD.

Q

QADHF See FALSE ALLEGATION OF UNCHASTITY

QALĀ'ID See SYMBOLS OF GOD

QARḌ ḤASAN See GOOD LOAN

QASAM See OATH

QIBLAH

Qiblah is the "direction" in which Muslims face while offering *ṣalāt* (*q.v.*).

I. Change of the Qiblah. As long as they were in Makkah, Muḥammad and his followers could perform *ṣalāt* facing Jerusalem and the Ka^{c}bah simultaneously. This no longer remained possible after the Emigration (*q.v.*), for Jerusalem is to the north, and the Ka^{c}bah to the south, of Madīnah. For about a year and a half, Jerusalem was the *qiblah* of the Muslims in Madīnah. Then a revelation instructed them to change their *qiblah* to the Ka^{c}bah.

The change of the *qiblah* was significant in that it further marked off the Muslims as a community with its own rituals and symbols. The change is presented by the Qur'ān as something that Muḥammad had looked forward to. 2:144 reads: "We have been watching you turning your face toward the sky. We shall, therefore, make you turn toward a *qiblah* of your liking. So turn your face toward the Sacred Mosque [*q.v.*]. . . ." To the question, Why was Muḥammad expecting a change in the *qiblah*, the following answer may be given.

In matters on which he had received no revelation, Muḥammad used to follow the practice of earlier prophets. In offering *ṣalāt*, he initially faced in the direction of Jerusalem, though, as noted above, in Makkah it was possible to face both Jerusalem and the Kaᶜbah at the same time. The inability, in Madīnah, to face the Kaᶜbah was painful for Muḥammad, and he waited for a revelation that would solve the problem. The revelation came about two months before the Battle of Badr (624).

II. The Change as a Test. 2:143 presents the change of the *qiblah* as a test from God; the change was made "in order that We may mark off those who follow the Messenger from those who will go back on their heels." The verse implies that the ranks of Muslims at that time included some former Jews and Christians who were still not entrenched in the new faith they had adopted. The change of the *qiblah* put their loyalties to a severe test. Purporting to cut them off emotionally from a longstanding ritual and tradition, it forced them to make a choice: they had to prove their unswerving loyalty to Muḥammad by accepting the new *qiblah*, or they had to renounce Islam, which is termed in the verse "going back on one's heels."

See also: ṢALĀT.

QIṢĀṢ

I. General. The usual translation of *qiṣāṣ* is "retaliation," but it is not very accurate. It is difficult to provide a good translation in English, and so the Arabic word will be retained in this article. According to the Qur'ānic understanding of the term, *qiṣāṣ* may be described as: just and merited punishment meted out, through the agency of a properly constituted legal authority, for murder (or injuries). A killer is punished because he destroys a life, violating a person's right to life; punishment for such a violation makes *qiṣāṣ* "merited." *Qiṣāṣ* cannot be in excess of the crime committed (2:178); this stipulation makes *qiṣāṣ* "just." The injunction of taking *qiṣāṣ* is given to the Muslim community as a whole, as is clear from 2:178–179; this in practical terms implies that the law of *qiṣāṣ* must be enforced by "a properly constituted legal authority."

II. Details. Several verses give details concerning *qiṣāṣ*. 2:178–179 read: "Believers, you have been placed under an obligation to take *qiṣāṣ*—a freeman for a freeman, a slave for a slave, and a woman for a woman. If he [killer] is then shown a measure of lenience by his brother, then the prevalent custom must be observed and payment made to him [survivor or relative of the person killed] . . . In *qiṣāṣ* there is life for you, O people of wisdom, so that you may achieve *taqwā* [see *piety*]." According to these verses, (a) it is the killer who shall be punished, a stipulation that eliminated the discrimination made in pre-Islamic Arabia in matters of *qiṣāṣ* between, for example, persons of high and low social ranks; (b) the right to waive *qiṣāṣ* rests with the aggrieved party; and (c) if *qiṣāṣ* is waived, the killer shall pay bloodwit. As for the statement, "In *qiṣāṣ* there is life for you," it is explained by 5:32: One who wrongfully kills an individual kills, as if it were, the entire mankind; and one who saves (literally, "revives") an individual from being killed, saves, as if it were, the whole humanity.

5:45 reads: "And we made the following incumbent upon them [Israelites]: A life for a life, an eye for an eye, a nose for a nose, an ear for an ear, and a tooth for a tooth; and for injuries, *qiṣāṣ*." This verse makes reference to one of the injunctions in the Torah (Exod. 21:23–25; Lev. 24:20; Deut. 19:21). In so referring to the injunction, and giving no indication that it has been repealed (see *abrogation*), the

Qur'ān retains the injunction as valid for the Muslim community as well.

See also: BLOODWIT.

QISSĪS

5:82 says that Christians are the most affectionate toward Muslims because there are, among them, "priests" (*qissīsīn*; sing. *qissīs*) and "monks" (*ruhbān*; see *monasticism*), and because they are not proud. The word *qissīs* was used by Christian Arabs for a (Christian) religious scholar.

See also: ḤIBR; MONASTICISM; RABBĀNĪ.

QITĀL See JIHĀD

QUR'ĀN

I. Name. The Qur'ān is the book containing the revelations received by Muḥammad. The Arabic word *qur'ān* is a verbal noun meaning "reading, recitation." It is often used in the Qur'ān with the definite article, which implies that it is *the* reading, or reading *par excellence.* Sometimes it is used without the definite article, and the indefiniteness implies "magnification," the meaning being that the Qur'ān is a great and valuable book. In 15:91 the word is used for the Torah, the "Qur'ān" of Jews.

II. Description. The Qur'ān is described as a book from God. It is not a fabrication of Muḥammad's (10:15, 37; 52:33–34); in fact human beings are not capable of producing a book like it—not even the combined efforts of the *jinn* (*q.v.*) and humans can produce a discourse like it (2:23–24; 10:38; 11:13–14; 17:88). It is ᶜ*aẓīm* ("great, magnificent"; 15:87), *karīm* ("noble"; 56:77), *majīd* ("eminent, illustrious"; 50:1; 85:21), *ḥakīm* ("full of wisdom"; 36:2; also 54:5), *mubīn* ("self-manifest"; 15:1; 27:1; 36:69), and *dhū* *dh-dhikr* ("serving to remind [mankind]"; 38:1). Being from God, it is free from inconsistencies or contradictions (4:82). It was revealed in Arabic so that it might be fully understood by its original addressees, the Arabs (12:2; 20:113; 26:195; 39:28; 41:3; 42:7; 43:3; also 14:4; 26:198–199; 41:44). It is "an admonition . . . and a cure for the maladies of the heart" (10:57; also 17:82). It is "the best discourse" (39:23). It guides to the Right Path (*q.v.*), giving good tidings to those who believe in it (17:9). It is the criterion for telling truth from falsehood (see *the criterion*). It contains the essence of the earlier scriptures, provides a criterion for evaluating those scriptures (*muhaymin*; 5:48), and is an "objectification" or "realization" (which, rather than "confirmation," is the correct meaning of the Qur'ānic term *taṣdīq* in 2:41, 89, 91, 97, 101; 3:3, 81; 4:47; 5:48; 6:92; 35:31; 46:30; 61:6) of the promises and predictions made in the earlier scriptures. It is ideally suitable (*taysīr* [literally, "to facilitate"]) for taking "remembrance" (*q.v.*; 54:17, 22, 32, 40). It has been made secure against corruption (41:41–42; also 15:9).

III. Method and Period of Revelation. The Qur'ānic revelations span a period of twenty-three years, from 610 (when Muḥammad announced his prophecy) to 632 (the year of his death). According to 2:185, the Qur'ān was revealed in the month of Ramaḍān (*q.v.*). This may mean that the revelation of the Qur'ān began in that month, or that the whole of the Qur'ān was revealed from the highest to the lowest heaven in that month and was from then onward revealed to Muḥammad as occasion demanded. The Qur'ān was revealed in parts so that it may be properly understood and reflected on (17:106; see also 25:32).

From 610 to 622 Muḥammad was in Makkah, and the revelations received by him during that period are known as the Makkan revelations; from 622 to 632 he was in Madīnah, and the revelations that came to him during that period are called the Madīnan revelations. Sūrahs containing predominantly Makkan revelations are termed Makkan, even if they have some Madīnan material in them. Similarly, sūrahs containing predominantly Madīnan revelations are called Madīnan.

IV. Contents. The Qur'ān deals with a vast number of subjects—creedal, ethical, philosophical, metaphysical, social, political, and economic—and many of them have been treated under appropriate heads in the present work. Broadly speaking, the contents of the Qur'ān may be divided into two categories: doctrine and conduct. The Makkan sūrahs deal mainly with matters of doctrine—e.g. *tawḥid* (see *monotheism*), prophecy (*q.v.*) and the hereafter (*q.v.*)—while the Madīnan sūrahs deal mainly with matters of conduct—e.g. *zakāt* (*q.v.*), inheritance (see *inheritance, law of*), marriage (*q.v.*), and marriage (*q.v.*).

V. Muḥkamāt and Mutashābihāt. From a certain point of view, the verses of the Qur'ān may be divided into two types: *muḥkamāt* and *mutashābihāt* (3:7). The *muḥkamāt* (literally, "firm ones") are said to be those verses which present self-evident truths, incontestable ethical norms, and established principles of truth, justice, and good conduct. The *mutashābihāt* (literally, "ambiguous ones") are verses which speak of a realm of existence that is beyond our ken (e.g. the hereafter [*q.v.*], paradise [see *heaven*], and hell [*q.v.*]), using such modes of speech as similes, metaphors, and similitudes. 3:7 calls the *muḥkamāt* the "mother" of the Qur'ān, meaning that they are the foundation of the Qur'ān and should principally occupy one's attention (see *umm al-kitāb*). Those who are interested in making mischief are, the verse says, mainly interested in the *mutashābihāt*; these people, that is to say, ignore the *muḥkamāt*, which furnish sure guidance, and instead split hairs with regard to the *mutashābihāt*.

VI. Structure. The generally held view about the Qur'ān, namely, that it lacks coherence and is disjointed, has been rejected by a number of modern Muslim scholars, who have sought to prove that the Qur'ān is marked by a remarkable coherence that is both hermeneutically significant and aesthetically pleasing.

VII. Style. Generally speaking, the Makkan sūrahs are more poetic and rhetorical whereas the Madīnan sūrahs are more discursive and matter-of-fact. Each type of style is suited to the revelations for which it is used. Elements of either type of style are, however, found in the other.

A few of the stylistic features of the Qur'ān may be noted. The language of the Qur'ān is marked by brevity and succinctness, which calls for close attention to such aspects of its style as ellipsis. In consonance with the standard Arabic style of its time, the Qur'ān employs *saj*[c] ("rhymed prose"), but, departing from the Arabian practice, does not make thought subservient to *saj*[c]. *Taṣrīf* (17:41, 89; 18:54; 20:113) is not simply "repetition," but "treatment of a subject from various angles." The same themes are brought up again and again, but, as a rule, are each time viewed from a different angle; "variegation" is perhaps a more accurate translation of *taṣrīf*. Similes and metaphors are frequently employed. The Qur'ān contains a rich dramatic element; Ss. 12 and 20 have some intensely dramatic episodes. It also makes use of irony, with S. 12 providing some remarkable examples of it.

VIII. Etiquette of Qur'ān Recitation. Before beginning recitation of the Qur'ān, one should seek the refuge of God against Satan (*q.v.*). If the Qur'ān is being recited, one should listen to it in respectful silence (7:204; also 46:29).

See also: ABROGATION; KITĀB; MIRACLE; NIGHT OF DECREE, THE; REVELATION.

QURBĀN See SACRIFICE

R

RABB

Rabb has two meanings: "nourisher, sustainer, provident being," and "master, lord." The second meaning arose from the first since only one who nourishes or sustains has the right to be master or lord. Usage, however, has made the second meaning the primary one, so that the word does not now mean "nourisher" or "sustainer" to the exclusion of the other meaning. God is the *rabb* of the whole universe (1:1; 2:131). Man, too, must accept Him as his *rabb* (6:164), for his proper role is that of an ᶜ*abd* (*q.v.*) to Him.

By combining the two meanings of *rabb*, the Qur'ān often makes the word the basis of an argument: God, Who is the sustainer of mankind, ought to be worshipped as the only true Lord. 3:51 reads: "Indeed, God is my [Jesus'] *rabb* and yours, so worship Him; this is the Right Path" (*q.v.*; see also 5:72, 117; 19:36; 26:26; 37:126; 43:64). The providence of God is thus one of the proofs the Qur'ān offers to establish the oneness of God.

See also: ᶜABD; WORSHIP.

RABBĀNĪ

Rabbānī (pl. *rabbāniyyūn*) literally means "one who is devoted to God," and is used in this sense in 3:79, which says that a prophet does not invite his people to worship him, but to worship God, asking them to become *rabbāniyyūn*. The "prophet" referred to is Jesus, and the criticism is aimed at Christians. In 5:44 the word occurs (in the plural) in conjunction with *aḥbār* (see *ḥibr*), and means "religious scholar." The verse praises those scholars of the Torah who were true followers of the Torah and who passed judgments in accordance with it. 5:63 criticizes those *rabbāniyyūn* (and also *aḥbār*) who did not stop their people from speaking falsehood and usurping other people's property.

3:146 uses the word *ribbī* (pl. *ribbiyyūn*), another form of *rabbānī*, saying that there have been many *ribbiyyūn* who have fought on the side of prophets and did not lose heart upon suffering hardship in the course of their struggle. The word seems to have been used in the same sense in which *rabbānī* is used in 3:79 (see above), and the verse seeks to console and encourage the Muslims who had suffered a setback in the Battle of Uḥud (625).

See also: ḤIBR; MONASTICISM; QISSĪS.

RAḌĀᶜAH See SUCKLING

RAHBĀNIYYAH See MONASTICISM

RĀHIB See MONASTICISM

RAMAḌĀN

Ramaḍān is the month of fasting (*q.v.*). It is the ninth month of the lunar calendar. It was during Ramaḍāan that the Qur'ān (*q.v.*) was revealed (2:185).

See also: FASTING.

RAMY See FALSE ALLEGATION OF UNCHASTITY

RASŪL See PROPHET

RECOMPENSE

Arabic: *jazā'*.

Recompense for actions is a basic theme in the Qur'ān (*q.v.*). Every action performed by human beings has a positive or negative moral value and will be given due recompense by God in the next world (40:17; 45:28; 53:41; 77:41–44; see *the hereafter*), though recompense may be given in this world as well (12:22; 16:30; 28:14; 46:25; 68:17–20).

Individuals will receive their complete recompense in the hereafter (see 6:94). As for nations, they are recompensed in this world in accordance with the laws of rise and fall of nations laid down by God.

See also: ACCOUNTABILITY; HEREAFTER, THE; HEAVEN; HELL; PUNISHMENT; REWARD.

RELIGION See DĪN

REMEMBRANCE

Arabic: *dhikr*.

Literally "remembrance, reminder," *dhikr* (also *dhikrā, tadhkirah*) is an important term in the Qur'ān. While it does not exactly coincide with the Platonic theory of knowledge as recollection (though a comparison may be instructive) *dhikr*, used of scriptures, signifies that the divine message "reminds" man of truths that lie deeply embedded in the human mind or soul. The thrust of the concept is that religion (see *dīn*) does not impose on man things from the outside but only taps the reservoir of faith and belief latent in man, exercising a formal influence upon that reservoir and channelizing it properly. The Qur'ān is described as *dhikr* (e.g. 15:9; 16:44; 21:50; 38:8; 41:41), and the People of the Book (*q.v.*) are called *ahl adh-dhikr* ("Possessors of the Reminder," i.e. of Scripture) in 16:43 and 21:7.

See also: COVENANT; DĪN; FIṬRAH.

REPENTANCE

Arabic: *tawbah.*

Repentance wipes off sins. But, in order for repentance to be effective, it must be made in a state of belief, and not in a state of disbelief or apostasy (3:90; 4:18; 33:73), must be accompanied by the will to mend one's ways and followed by good actions (2:160; 3:89; 5:39; 6:54; 7:153; 19:60; 20:82; 24:5; 25:71; 28:67), and should occur without delay (4:17). Sincere repentance may even lead to the turning of bad actions into good actions (25:70). Also, sins committed "in heedlessness" will be forgiven upon repentance, but not sins committed brazenly and persistently 4:17–18). The believers are asked to make *tawbah naṣūḥ* ("sincere repentance"; 66:8). God is greatly accepting of repentance (2:37, 54, 128, 160; 4:16, 64; 9:104, 118; 24:10; 49:12; 110:3), and He loves those who are truly repentant (2:222).

Adam, after he had sinned, repented and was forgiven by God (2:37). Thus he was sent upon earth not to receive punishment for his disobedience, but in accordance with an already existing plan. Since Adam was forgiven, no original sin attaches to the human race (see *man*).

See also: ATONEMENT; FORGIVENESS.

RESPITE

Arabic: *imhāl; imlā'.*

"To give respite" is "to give rope": instead of punishing the wicked and the disbelieving immediately, God gives them respite (13:32; 16:61; 35:45). The respite is meant to serve two purposes. First, it presents one with an opportunity to abandon one's wicked ways and reform oneself. The people of Jonah turned to God at the last minute, averting punishment (10:98). Second, it allows a man, or a people, to commit as many sins as the individual or the nation wishes to, so that the punishment, when it comes, is complete and unsparing (3:178). Delay in punishment does not mean that God is unable to inflict the punishment; God's strategem is effective and He closes in on the wicked, unbeknownst to them (7:182–183; 22:44, 48; 68:44–45).

See also: PUNISHMENT.

RESURRECTION See HEREAFTER, THE; HOUR, THE

RETALIATION See QIṢĀṢ

REVELATION

Arabic: *waḥy*.

I. **Meanings.** *Waḥy* has several meanings in the Qur'ān:

1. *Gesture.* Zechariah's inability to speak for three days was a sign that he would be blessed with a son. So, upon meeting people, he "motioned" to them to glorify God day and night (19:10–11). The meaning of the word in 99:5 is essentially the same.

2. *Natural instinct.* The bee is equipped with the instinct to make honey (16:68–69). A closely related meaning is found in 41:12: upon creating the heavens, God "revealed" to every heaven the command peculiar to it, i.e. promulgated a certain set of laws in it.

3. *Inspired Thought.* Moses' mother was instructed by God to cast the infant Moses in the sea in case she feared for his life (28:7; also 20:38). The disciples of Jesus (see *ḥawārī*) were similarly inspired by God (5:111). Satans (see *Satan*) inspire their followers with evil thoughts (6:121) and false hopes (6:112).

4. *Message of Guidance.* Every prophet (*q.v.*) receives from God a message which he conveys to his people in order to guide them to the Right Path (*q.v.*). "Revelation" is the technical name for such a message. The following paragraphs deal principally with *waḥy* in this sense.

II. Modes of Revelation. 42:51 describes three ways in which revelation is given. The first is inspiration. But this inspiration is to be distinguished from "inspired thought," mentioned above, in that 42:51 calls it a form of "speech" (see below). The second is revelation given "from behind a veil." Moses wanted to see God, but was unable to, though God spoke to him unseen by him (4:164; 7:143–144). The third form, according to 42:51, is the message conveyed to the heart of the prophet by an angel (also 2:97).

There are two other ways in which man receives divine communication. An angel may assume human form and communicate a message from God to a prophet. Thus angels came and spoke to Abraham (11:70; 29:31–32) and Lot (11:81; 29:33–34). Mary, though not a prophet, was spoken to by angels (3:42–43, 45–49), as was Abraham's wife (11:72–73). Sometimes revelation may come to a prophet in the form of a vision (*ru'yā*), as it did to Abraham, who was instructed to sacrifice his son (37:102; see *sacrifice*), and to Muḥammad (see *ascension*).

III. Nature of Revelation. Does revelation (in the sense of "message of guidance") take the form of verbal or non-verbal communication? The Qur'ān seems to suggest that it is verbal. The inspiration of which 42:51 speaks is a form of speech, and speech suggests words. The second mode of revelation mentioned in the verse is obviously verbal, as is the mode in which angels in human form communicate a message to a prophet. As for the two other modes (conveying of a message to a prophet's heart, and *ru'yā*), they do not necessarily exclude the possibility of a verbal communication.

Also, the revelation given to Muḥammad is in 42:7 called "an Arabic reading" (*qur'ānan ᶜarabiyyan*). "Reading" implies words (in 75:16–19 Muḥammad is instructed not to move his tongue in haste in *reading* the Qur'ān but to follow the *reading* of it by God; the word "reading" in this verse is a physical act, again implying the utterance of *words*), while the use of the word "Arabic" implies that revelation was given in a particular language (see 14:4)—that is to say, in *words*. Finally, we may note that one of the demands of the opponents of Muḥammad was that God speak to them. The demand, obviously, was meant to contradict the Prophet's claim that God "spoke" to him—that is, communicated to him using words.

The Qur'ān, therefore, would seem to support the notion of the objectivity or otherness of revelation. 85:21–22 say that the Qur'ān is part of the record contained in the "Preserved Tablet" (*q.v.*), and the expression is meant, among other things, to establish the otherness of the revelation. The revelation given to Moses possessed the same objectivity since it was given in the form of tablets with commandments inscribed on it (7:145).

IV. Revelation as Life. 42:52 calls revelation "spirit" (*rūḥ*), implying that revelation, or divine guidance, is "life" for those who follow the revelation.

See also: QUR'ĀN.

REWARD

Arabic: *thawāb*.

Good actions will earn their reward in the hereafter, and the reward will be in the form of paradise (see *heaven*; 3:195; 5:85; 18:46.) The reward for good actions is at least ten-fold (6:160).

See also: ACCOUNTABILITY; HEREAFTER, THE; PUNISHMENT; RECOMPENSE.

RIBĀ See INTEREST

RIBBĪ See RABBĀNĪ

RIGHT PATH, THE

Arabic: *aṣ-ṣirāṭ al-mustaqīm.*

The Right Path is that which leads straight to God (11:56). Several verses identify it as belief in the One God and worship of Him. In 7:16 Satan challenges God, saying that he will turn mankind away from the Right Path of God by teaching them to set up partners to Him. Jesus describes the path as worship of the One God (19:36; also 43:64). Muḥammad is said to be on the Right Path (36:3–4; 43:43) and guiding others to it (23:73; 42:52). Muslims are instructed to pray for guidance to the Right Path (1:5–6).

See also: MEDIAN COMMUNITY, THE.

RIGHTEOUSNESS See PIETY

RISĀLAH See PROPHECY

RITUAL PRAYER See ṢALĀT

RŪḤ See HOLY SPIRIT, THE; REVELATION

RŪH AL-AMĪN, AR- See HOLY SPIRIT, THE

RŪḤ AL-QUDUS, AR- See HOLY SPIRIT, THE

S

SĀᶜAH See HOUR, THE

SABEANS

Arabic: *ṣābi'ūn.*

It appears that the Sabeans were well known as a religious group in the times of Muḥammad, so that a simple reference (2:62; 5:69) to them was sufficient to identify them. But since they no longer exist, it is difficult to say anything about them with certainty. The Qur'ānic description of them leads one to think that in the beginning they followed a revealed religion but that, with the passage of time, their religion became corrupted. Tradition knows them as worshippers of angels and stars. It is conceivable that, as a result of religious and moral corruption, they began to worship stars and angels.

ṢABR See PERSEVERANCE

SACRED HOUSE, THE See SACRED MOSQUE, THE

SACRED LAND, THE See SACRED MOSQUE, THE

SACRED LANDMARK, THE

Arabic: *al-mash^{c}ar al-ḥarām.*

Muzdalifah, which is situated between Makkah and ^{c}Arafāt, is called "the Sacred Landmark" in 2:198. The pilgrims of *ḥajj* (see *pilgrimage*) are required to leave Makkah for ^{c}Arafāt on the 9th of Dhū l-Ḥijjah and, on their way back the following day, to spend the night at Muzdalifah. In pre-Islamic times, the pilgrims held meetings at Muzdalifah in which poetry was recited, stories were told, and the feats of tribes and ancestors were trumpted. 2:198 enjoins the pilgrims to abandon that pagan custom. Muzdalifah, the verse says, is a religious landmark, and so the pilgrims should, during their stay there, spend their time in remembrance of God.

SACRED MONTHS, THE

Arabic: *ash-shahr al-ḥarām.*

From the time of Abraham, four months (Dhū l-Qa^{c}dah, Dhū l-Ḥijjah, Muḥarram, and Rajab) were regarded as "the Sacred Months" (2:194, 217; 5:2, 97; 9:5); the first three were the months of *ḥajj* (see *pilgrimage*), and the last the month of *^{c}umrah* (see *pilgrimage*). During these months it was strictly forbidden to wage war, loot, or plunder. Islam maintained the prohibition, but made observance of the months by Muslims contingent upon observance of them by their opponents, the Quraysh. 2:194 says, "Sacred months are in return for sacred months," i.e. are to be held sacred only if they are held sacred by the opponents.

SACRED MOSQUE, THE

Arabic: *al-masjid al-ḥarām.*

The Ka^{c}bah (*q.v.*) is called "the sacred mosque" in many verses (2:144, 149, 150, 191, 196, 217; 5:2; 8:34;

9:7, 19, 28; 17:1; 22:25; 48:25, 27). Elsewhere it is called "the sacred house" (*al-bayt al-ḥarām* [5:2, 97] and *al-bayt al-muḥarram* [14:37]). Because of the Ka^{c}bah, the land of Makkah is called "the sacred land" (*al-baldah al-muḥarramah*; 27:91).

See also: ANCIENT HOUSE, THE; DISTANT MOSQUE, THE; PILGRIMAGE; SANCTUARY OF PEACE, THE.

SACRIFICE

Arabic: *hady; mansak, nusuk; qurbān.*

I. Sacrifice as Ritual. The pilgrims of *ḥajj* (see *pilgrimage*) are required to make animal sacrifice during the *ḥajj*. Sacrifice is offered at Minā on the 10th of Dhū l-Ḥijjah. If one does not have the means to offer animal sacrifice, one should fast a certain number of days (see *atonement*).

The institution of animal sacrifice (*mansak*) has been a part of every dispensation that has come to mankind from God (22:34). The Muslim ritual of sacrifice is thus a continuation of an earlier religious tradition, though it also perpetuates the memory of Abraham's remarkable loyalty to God. When he was commanded in a dream to sacrifice his son, Abraham unflinchingly carried out the command, but God saved the son "by means of a great sacrifice" (37:102–107), that is, a ram.

The animals that may be sacrificed during the *ḥajj* are *bahīmat al-an^{c}ām* (5:1), that is, camels, cows, sheep, and goats (6:142–144), and similar other animals. Sacrificial animals are counted among the "symbols of God" (*q.v.*; 5:2; 22:36).

II. Burnt Offering as Proof of Prophecy. 3:183 refers to the Madīnan Jews' claim that God had enjoined them not to accept anyone as prophet until he had presented the miracle of burnt offering. The Bible records incidents in which the burnt offering was presented as sacrifice by prophets and others, but does not say that such an offering is proof of the veracity of a claimant to prophecy. On the contrary, it records incidents in which the Israelites threatened to kill prophets (like Elijah the Tishbite) who did present the burnt offering (I Kg. 18–19). 3:183 alludes to such incidents: "There have come to you before me [Muḥammad] prophets who presented manifest proofs, and also the proof you speak of [i.e. miracle of burnt offering]; so why did you kill them if you are telling the truth [regarding the criterion for accepting a prophet]?"

ṢADAQAH

Ṣadaqah (roughly, "charity") is of two types: mandatory and optional. The latter will be discussed below; for the former, see *zakāt*.

Ṣadaqah may be given publicly or secretly (2:271). Giving it publicly has the advantage of setting an example for others and inducing them to give *ṣadaqah*; it is especially useful when people are to be exhorted to make financial contributions for an important social cause. Giving *ṣadaqah* secretly has the merit of performing a good act without ostentation and of helping the poor and the needy (*q.v.*) without hurting their self-respect. In either case, *ṣadaqah* must not be followed with hurt or a condescending attitude (see *condescension*) toward the recipient of it, for that will deprive the *ṣadaqah* of reward in the hereafter (2:263–264).

Ṣadaqah is one of the principal forms of making atonement (*q.v.*). It is also a test of sincerity (see *najwā*).

See also: ATONEMENT; CONDESCENSION; SPENDING IN THE WAY OF GOD; NAJWĀ; ZAKĀT.

ṢADUQAH See DOWER

ṢAGHĪRAH See MAJOR SIN AND MINOR SIN

ṢĀḤIB BI L-JANB, AṢ- See CHANCE COMPANION

SĀ'IBAH See ANIMAL VENERATION

SĀ'IL See NEEDY, THE

SALĀM See GREETING

ṢALĀT

I. General. *Ṣalāt* (roughly, "ritual prayer") is the obligatory prayer a Muslim offers five times a day following certain fixed rules. The Qur'ān suggests that all prophets performed *ṣalāt* and instructed their followers to do so (11:87; 14:40; 19:31, 55), though the actual form of *ṣalāt* may have differed from one age to another. The Qur'ān criticizes the Jews for having "wasted," i.e. neglected, *ṣalāt* (19:59; see also 2:43, 83), and castigates the pagan Arabs for reducing *ṣalāt* to a set of ludicrous rituals (8:35).

II. Pillar of Islam. *Ṣalāt* is the first and foremost "pillar" of Islam, and the Qur'ān instructs Muslims to "establish" and "protect" it (e.g. 2:110, 238; 6:92; 23:9; 70:23, 34), that is, to perform it with regularity and care. *Ṣalāt* must be made under nearly all circumstances, even when one is on a journey or in battle, though in these cases it may be shortened (4:101–102). One of the few exceptions made (in *Ḥadīth*) is for a menstruating woman, who is exempted from performing *ṣalāt* during her period. Ablution (*q.v.*) has to be made before performing *ṣalāt* (5:6).

III. Timings. The timings of *ṣalāt* are fixed (4:103). On one interpretation, 50:39–40 gives the timings of all the five prayers (dawn, noon, late-afternoon, sunset, night). Elsewhere some of the prayers are mentioned by name: the dawn prayer (*ṣalāt al-fajr*; 24:58; also 17:78); the night prayer (*ṣalāt al-ᶜishā'*; 24:58); the late-afternoon prayer (*aṣ-ṣalāt al-wusṭā* (2:238). The optional late-night prayer, known as *ṣalāt at-tahajjud*, finds mention in 17:79.

IV. Friday Prayer. On Friday, the second prayer of the day must be performed in a mosque congregationally (62:9), unless a genuine excuse exists. The addressees of the injunction are taken to be (adult) Muslim males; women may join the prayer in the mosque, but are not required to. At the call for the Friday prayer, all economic activity must cease and preparations for the *ṣalāt* begun; economic activity may be resumed after the prayer (62:9–10).

V. Impact of Ṣalāt. *Ṣalāt* is a source of strength in times of difficulty (2:45, 153), and it guards one against immorality (29:45; also 31:17). The people of the prophet Shuᶜayb criticized Shuᶜayb, saying: "Does your *ṣalāt* command you [concerning us] that we abandon what our ancestors worshipped, or that we do with our wealth what we like?" (11:87). The verse implies that *ṣalāt*, properly performed, has definite behavioral implications: since it is performed for God alone, it forbids one to set up partners to God (see *idolatry*); and it induces one to spend of one's wealth in the way of God (see *spending in the way of God*).

See also: PRAYER.

ṢALĀT AL-FAJR See ṢALĀT

ṢALĀT AL-ᶜISHĀ' See ṢALĀT

ṢALĀT AL-WUSṬĀ, AS- See ṢALĀT

ṢALĀT AT-TAHAJJUD See ṢALĀT

ṢĀLIḤ See GOOD ACTION

SALVATION

Arabic: *falāḥ; fawz.*

Salvation in the hereafter is the ultimate goal of man;

one who achieves that goal attains real success (4:13; 6:16; 59:20; 61:12), while one who fails to achieve it has failed completely (8:37; 22:11; 39:15).

Salvation depends on good actions (22:77), a fairly representative list of which is to be found in 23:1–11 and 70:22–35. But, as 23:1–11 indicate, good actions include acts of social as well as personal virtue. Since good actions originate from the goodness of the heart, purity of the self is sometimes described as ensuring salvation (87:14; 91:9).

See also: FAITH; GOOD ACTION; HEAVEN.

SALWĀ See MANN AND SALWĀ

SANCTUARY OF PEACE, THE

Arabic: *ḥaram āmin.*

The city of Makkah is called a "sanctuary of peace" (28:57; 29:67). Before Abraham built the Ka^c^bah (*q.v.*), Makkah, like the rest of Arabia, lacked peace and security (28:57; 29:67). Abraham prayed to God that the city be made, because of the Ka^c^bah, a "city of peace" (2:126; 14:35; also 95:3). That Makkah was thus blessed is described in S. 106 as one of God's special favors to the Quraysh, who are asked to show gratitude for the favor by worshipping the Lord of the Ka^c^bah alone.

See also: SACRED MOSQUE, THE.

SARIQAH See THEFT

SATAN

Arabic: *shayṭān* (pl. *shayāṭīn*).

I. Not a Distinct Species. *Shayṭān* literally means "reckless, headstrong, defiant, violent." There does not exist a satanic species as such; rather, those from among men and *jinn* (*q.v.*) who defy God become satans (6:112; also

2:14). Iblīs, who refused to bow to Adam, was a *jinn* who disobeyed God's commandment (18:50), and his disobedience made him a satan. He is usually referred to in the Qur'ān as *ash-shayṭān* (*the* satan, or Satan). All those who choose to follow Satan's path become his "progeny" (18:50), "party" (58:19) or "friends" (4:76). The *jinn* in Solomon's service were satan *jinn* (21:82; 34:14; 38:37). In 2:14 the word *shayāṭīn* is used for the leading opponents of Muḥammad.

II. Satans as Enemies of Humans. Satans are the sworn enemies of man (7:22; 12:5; 17:53; 35:6; 43:62). It was a satan *jinn*, Iblīs, who misled Adam and Eve (2:35). Satans have tried to thwart the mission of every prophet and messenger, though their attempts are frustrated by God (22:52; also 6:112).

III. Satans' Strategy. Satans do not have direct control over man. Rather, they use the method of insinuation and suggestion (*wiswās* [7:20; 20:120] and *hamazāt* [23:97]). They try to mislead man by painting evil and wrong in bright colors (*tazyīn*: 6:43; 8:48; 16:63; 27:24; 29:38; *taswīl*: 47:25) and making attractive but false promises (*ghurūr*: 4:120; 17:64). But when man does commit an evil act, they wash their hands of him; they are the "great betrayers" (25:29; also 59:16). In the hereafter, too, they will exonerate themselves of all responsibility for misguiding man, arguing that they enjoyed no real power over man, that they simply invited man to commit evil and man chose to do so (14:22).

Certain acts are called "satanic": wine-drinking and gambling (5:90–91; see *wine and game of chance*); immorality (*q.v.*) and *munkar* (see *enjoining good and forbidding evil*); and extravagant spending of wealth (17:27; see *extravagance*).

IV. Defense against Satanic Attacks. The best defense against satanic attacks is to pray to God and seek refuge in Him (7:200–201; 41:36). One should also seek the refuge of God against Satan before beginning the recitation of the Qur'ān (*q.v.*; 16:98).

See also: ENVY; EVIL; JINN.

SAWĀ' AS-SABĪL See MEDIAN COMMUNITY, THE

ṢAWM See FASTING

SCALES, THE See MĪZĀN

SCRIPTURE See KITĀB

SEAL OF THE PROPHETS, THE

Arabic: *khātam an-nabiyyīn.*

Muḥammad is called "the seal of the prophets" in 33:40. The expression means that Muḥammad is the final prophet, and that the institution of prophecy after him is "sealed."

See also: PROPHECY; PROPHET.

SEALING

Arabic: *khatm; ṭab^{c}; izāghah.*

When a man, through repeated acts of sin, vitiates the inherent goodness of his nature (see *fiṭrah*) and becomes utterly evil, God seals off his heart, ears, and eyes, so that he becomes incapable of receiving the truth and taking the Right Path (*q.v.*; 2:6–7; 4:155; 7:100–101; 16:106–108; 18:57; 30:59; 40:35; 45:23; 63:3). Only he who deserves it is punished with "sealing." As 61:5 says: "When they became crooked, God made their hearts crooked." Moses prayed to God to seal off the hearts of Pharaoh and his nobility so that they should become incapable of believing before they actually see the promised punishment descending upon them (10:88). The sealing is thus a punishment from God, the punishment in the hereafter being a natural result of this sealing.

See also: CURSE; FREEDOM AND PREDESTINATION; PUNISHMENT; SUNNAH OF GOD.

SHAᶜĀ'IR ALLĀH See SYMBOLS OF GOD

SHAFĀᶜAH See INTERCESSION

SHAHĀDAH See PHENOMENAL AND NON-PHENOMENAL REALMS, THE; WITNESS

SHAHĪD See WITNESS

SHAHR AL-ḤARĀM, ASH- See SACRED MONTHS, THE

SHAJARAH AL-MALᶜŪNAH, AL- See ACCURSED TREE, THE

SHARR See EVIL

SHAYṬĀN See SATAN

SHIRK See IDOLATRY

SHUKR See GRATITUDE

SHŪRĀ See CONSULTATION, PRINCIPLE OF

ṢIBGHAT ALLĀH See HUE OF GOD, THE

SIḤR See MAGIC

SIN See MAJOR SIN AND MINOR SIN

ṢIRĀṬ AL-MUSTAQĪM, AṢ- See RIGHT PATH, THE

ṢIYĀM See FASTING

SLAVERY

Slavery was widespread in Arabia at the time Islam made its advent. Abolition of slavery was part of the program of social reform envisaged by Islam. But, instead of abolishing overnight a deep-rooted institution and thus risking serious social dislocations, Islam took a graduated approach to the problem and laid down a detailed program for its solution.

I. Measures. The steps taken by Islam to eradicate slavery may be divided into two categories:

1. *Moral-Religious.* People were encouraged to free slaves, and emancipation of slaves was called a virtuous and commendable act (2:177; 90:13). Freeing of slaves was made one of the standard ways of atoning for sins and lapses (see *atonement*). 4:36 enjoins that slaves be treated kindly.

2. *Legal.* It was laid down that a slave could secure his freedom through *mukātabah* (24:33). *Mukātabah*, which may be translated "freedom contract," is the contract between a slave and his master to the effect that the master will free the slave in return for a given amount of money or performance of a stated service. The wording of 24:33 makes *mukātabah* at least highly recommeded, if not obligatory; it also instructs the Muslim community, or the Islamic State, to provide financial support to the slave in securing his freedom. "Freeing slaves" is one of the heads of expenditure of *zakāt* (*q.v.*; 9:60), which means that one of the responsibilities of an Islamic government is to help slaves win their freedom.

Another measure that led to the abolition of slavery was the recommendation to marry female slaves. If a man did not have the financial means to marry a freewoman, he was advised to marry a female Muslim slave, with the permission of her owner (4:25), since marriage with a female slave entailed fewer legal responsibilities.

II. War Captives. In pre-Islamic Arabia there were three types of slaves: freemen who were captured, made slaves, and sold for money; offspring of slaves who, like their parents, remained slaves; and war captives. Islam categorically abolished the first two types of slavery. As for war captives, they could be made slaves only if the enemy was unwilling to free Muslim prisoners of war in exchange for them. But the Islamic State is free to adopt any suitable policy in this connection.

Cohabitation with female slaves (*milk al-yamīn*) is allowed (23:6; 70:30). The law imposes several conditions, however. For example, cohabitation is allowed only if no arrangements can be made for the exchange of prisoners of war, and only those men may cohabit with them in whose possession they are given by the State. Today, at any rate, the issue of cohabitation with female slaves is of historical interest only.

See also: ATONEMENT.

SORCERY See MAGIC

SPENDING IN THE WAY OF GOD

Arabic: *infāq*.

Infāq ("spending") is the general word used for spending of wealth for social and communal causes. It includes both mandatory spending (see *zakāt*) and voluntary spending (see *ṣadaqah*), and is often an abbreviated form of *infāq fī sabīl Allāh* ("spending in the way of God").

The Qur'ān enjoins *infāq* upon Muslims. The beneficiaries of one's *infāq* (2:215) may be one's parents, relatives, orphans (see *orphan*), the needy (*q.v.*), and wayfarers (see *wayfarer*). One should spend of one's wealth freely because, first, the wealth one possesses is a gift from God (2:3; 4:39), and, second, because God will compensate for everything that is spent for His sake, repaying it manifold (2:261, 265). The Qur'ān praises those who spend of their wealth for good causes "in times of ease and difficulty" (3:134), "day and night, secretly and publicly" (2:274; also 13:22; 14:31; 16:75). But *infāq*, if it is to earn reward from God, must be motivated by the desire to please God (2:265, 272), and not by a wish to win popular acclaim (2:264). Also, the beneficiaries of *infāq* must not be caused any hurt or treated with contempt or condescension (*q.v.*; 2:262, 264). Special reward is promised for those who spend of their wealth in a social emergency (57:10). As can be seen, *infāq* can be an important means of eliminating economic disparities in society and meeting other social needs.

See also: ṢADAQAH; ZAKĀT.

SPIRIT See HOLY SPIRIT, THE; REVELATION

SPOILS

The spoils of war are of two types: movable property taken specifically from the enemy troops as a result of actual combat—these spoils are called *ghanā'im* (sing. *ghanīmah*); and movable and immovable property obtained from the enemy in circumstances not involving combat—these are called *fay'*. The distinction between the two types of spoils is made in 59:6.

I. Ghanā'im. The rules for the distribution of *ghanā'im* are laid down in 8:41. One-fifth of the *ghanā'im* are to be set aside for God, the Prophet, the relatives of the Prophet, orphans (see *orphan*), *masākīn* (see *the needy*), and wayfarers (see *wayfarer*); the rest is to be distributed among the troops who obtained the *ghanā'im*. The expression "for

God" means "for the purpose of promoting the Islamic religion." The Prophet was entitled to a portion of *ghanā'im* because, as the administrative head of the Muslim community, he devoted all his time and energies in looking after the community and had no spare time in which to earn a living for himself or for his family. The relatives of the Prophet were to receive a share because they were dependent upon the Prophet for their maintenance.

It is notable that *ghanā'im* are called *anfāl* in 8:1. *Nafal* (sing. of *anfāl*) literally means "surplus." When, after the Battle of Badr (624), the question of the distribution of spoils created an unpleasant situation, the Qur'ān sought to correct the outlook of Muslims. By using the word *anfāl* in 8:1, it suggested that the spoils were a "surplus" or a "gift" from God over which it did not behoove Muslims to bicker and quarrel. Only after correcting the outlook of Muslims did the Qur'ān come back, in 8:41, to the question of the distribution of spoils, this time calling them by their proper name, *ghanā'im*.

II. Fay'. After the expulsion of the Jewish tribe of Banū n-Naḍīr from Madīnah, the Muslims acquired *fay'*. According to 59:7–8, the *fay'*-spoils are for God (see above); the Prophet and his relatives (see above); orphans; *masākīn*; wayfarers; and people who have emigrated to the Islamic land (see *emigration*) and are in need. In other words, the *fay'*-spoils are not to be distributed among the troops who obtained them.

SUCKLING

Arabic: *raḍāᶜah*.

The relationship of suckling establishes a barrier to marriage: one cannot marry one's foster-mother or foster-sister (4:23).

If a father wants his children to be suckled by their mother after the couple are divorced, he can have the mother suckle the children for two years, but he must provide food and clothing to her during that period (2:223).

See also: LAWFUL AND THE UNLAWFUL, THE; MARRIAGE.

SULṬĀN See MANIFEST PROOF

SUNNAH OF GOD

The *sunnah* (literally, "path, way"; pl. *sunan*) of God is the "law" in accordance with which God deals with men and intervenes in history. The laws of God are rigorous and unchanging. The following are explicitly called the *sunan* of God:

1. *Triumph of Rasūl.* A *rasūl* (*q.v.*) must triumph over his opponents. If a people decisively rejects a *rasūl*, it cannot survive for long—an unchanging *sunnah* of God (17:76–77; 33:62; 35:43; 48:22–23). Since this *sunnah* was enforced in the case of nations previous to the Arabs, it is also called *sunnat al-awwalīn* ("the sunnah of earlier peoples"; 8:38; 15:13; 18:55; 35:43; also 3:137).

2. *Difficulties in Promoting the Truth.* A prophet faces difficulties in presenting his message before his people and in promoting the truth. But these difficulties are not meant to vex or disconcert the prophet; they are, rather, tests (see *trial*) to which all prophets are put in accordance with the *sunnah* of God (33:38).

3. *Irrevocableness of Punishment.* A disbelieving people that comes to believe only when punishment is about to descend upon it does not gain by its belief; God's *sunnah* for such a people is that it shall perish (40:84–85).

There are other *sunnahs* of God. Fluctuations of fortune are meant to put men to the test (see *trial*). And if a people consigns the verses of God to oblivion, God causes that people to forget those verses (see *abrogation*).

See also: SEALING; TRIAL.

SUPERSTITION See ANIMAL VENERATION; DIVINATION; JIBT

ṢŪR See TRUMPET, THE

SYMBOLS OF GOD

Arabic: *shaᶜā'ir Allāh.*

The "symbols of God" are things that make one "conscious" (*shaᶜā'ir*) of God or point to God. This being their function, they ought to be respected. The following are called the symbols of God, though obviously they do not exhaust the list: the mounts Ṣafā and Marwah (2:158), near Makkah; the sacred months (*q.v.*); animals sent to the Kaᶜbah as sacrificial offerings (*hady*) and "animals with [votive] collars around their necks" (*qalā'id*; 5:2).

See also: SACRED LANDMARK, THE; SACRED MONTHS, THE; SACRIFICE.

T

ṬAB[c] See SEALING

TABARRUJ See OSTENTATION

TABDHĪR See EXTRAVAGANCE

TADHKIRAH See REMEMBRANCE

TADHKIYAH See LAWFUL AND THE UNLAWFUL, THE

TĀBŪT See ARK OF THE COVENANT, THE

TAFRĪQ BAYN AR-RUSUL See DISCRIMINATION BETWEEN PROPHETS

ṬĀGHŪT

Ṭāghūt (literally, "one who has crossed the limits," hence: "rebel") is any power or being that rebels against God and demands loyalty and obedience over against the loyalty and obedience that is rightfully due to God alone.

Belief in God is irreconcilable with belief in the *ṭāghūt* (see 4:60); success and good tidings are for those who reject the *ṭāghūt* and serve God (2:256; 39:17; also 5:60). One can fight either in the way of God (see *jihād*) or in the way of the *ṭāghūt* (4:76). According to the verse, Satan makes use of the *ṭāghūt* in his attempt to misguide men.

Unlike God, Who leads men out of darkness and into light, the *ṭāghūt* lead men from light back into darkness (2:257; in this verse the word is used as a plural).

TAHLĪL See LAWFUL AND THE UNLAWFUL, THE

TAḤRĪF See DISTORTION OF SCRIPTURE

TAḤRĪM See LAWFUL AND THE UNLAWFUL, THE

TAKABBUR See PRIDE

TAKĀTHUR See COMPETITION

ṬALĀQ See DIVORCE

TANĀJĪ See NAJWĀ

TAQDĪS See GLORIFICATION OF GOD

TAQIYYAH See DISSIMULATION

TAQWĀ See PIETY

TASBĪḤ See GLORIFICATION OF GOD

TAṢDĪQ See QUR'ĀN

TASKHĪR See NATURE

TAṢRĪF See QUR'ĀN

TAWAKKUL See TRUST

TAWBAH See REPENTANCE

TAWBAH NAṢŪH See REPENTANCE

TAWḤĪD See MONOTHEISM

TAYAMMUM See DRY ABLUTION

TAYSĪR See FREEDOM AND DETERMINISM; QUR'ĀN

TESTIMONY See WITNESS

THAWĀB See REWARD

THEFT

Arabic: *sariqah*.

Theft is to be punished with the cutting off of the thief's hand (5:38). *Ḥadīth* and law place a number of limits on the infliction of the punishment, restricting the application of the word "theft" to acts committed under certain kinds of circumstances only.

THRONE

Arabic: *ᶜarsh; kursī*.

Of the two words used for the Throne of God, *kursī* occurs only once (2:255) and represents God's dominion or sovereignty: "His *kursī* extends over the heavens and the earth." The word *ᶜarsh* occurs many times, and although sometimes it, too, signifies "dominion" or "sovereignty" (as in 11:7), more often it denotes "throne" in a literal sense (e.g. 39:75; 69:17; 81:20). The expressions "Lord of the Throne" (*rabb al-ᶜarsh*; 21:22; 23:86) and "He of the Throne" (*dhū l-ᶜarsh*; 17:42; 40:15; 85:15) are susceptible of a metaphorical as well as a literal interpretation, though in most cases a literal interpretation would be preferable.

The expression *istiwā' ᶜalā l-ᶜarsh* ("to seat oneself on the throne"), used of God, means: to administer affairs, be in charge of matters (7:54; 10:3; 13:2; 20:5; 25:59; 32:4; 57:4). 10:3 brings out this meaning most clearly.

TRIAL

Arabic: *balā'; fitnah.*

I. General. According to the Qur'ān, life is a trial—more accurately, a series of trials. The very purpose of the creation of the heavens and the earth is described as putting man to the test (11:7), and the same purpose is attributed to the creation of life and death (67:2). In order to earn paradise (see *heaven*), therefore, one has to prove one's worth in the tests to which one will be put during one's life (2:155; 3:186; 23:30; 29:2–3). Trials set those who are truly faithful apart from those who are not (3:166–167, 179; 9:16; 29:3; 47:31).

II. Forms of Trial. Trial can take many forms. An individual or a nation may be tested through affluence, poverty, or suffering (8:28; 18:7; 20:131; 21:35; 64:15; also 6:165; 7:168; 23:55–56; 89:15–16); through a certain being, object, or event (6:53; 8:28; 9:126; 17:60; 21:35; 25:20; 64:15) or through loss of life and property, famine and starvation, injury and sickness, and ridicule of opponents (2:155, 214; 3:140–142, 186). Delay in punishment makes disbelievers even more skeptical, thus constituting another trial for them (21:109–111). Human beings may be a "trial" for one another. Thus the persecution of the believers by the unbelievers may put the faith of the former to a severe test (29:10); love of one's family may motivate one to break the commandments of God (8:28; 25:20; 64:14–15); and a pact between two nations may test the sincerity and commitment of both (16:92). The Qur'ān recounts a number of particular incidents which became a trial for men. For instance, the making of the golden calf became a trial for the Israelites (20:85), and the change of the *qiblah (q.v.)* became a trial for those who were weak in faith (2:143).

III. A Universal Principle. The rule of trial applies to all. That is, all human beings are tried. Not even prophets are an exception to the rule. Abraham, for instance, was tried through the dream in which he was instructed to slaughter his son (37:106), and Joseph was tempted by the sexual advances of Potiphar's wife (12:23–24). Those who succeed in a trial become stronger in their faith, those who fail go further astray (74:31).

See also: CALIPH; EVIL; FITNAH.

TRUMPET, THE

Arabic: *ṣūr.*

The Last Day will be brought about by the sound of the Trumpet. The Trumpet will be sounded twice. When it is first blown, its terrifying sound will knock people unconscious (39:68; also 27:87). At the second blowing, all people, the dead and the unconscious, will arise and assemble for judgment (39:68; also 18:89; 78:18). On the day of the blowing of the Trumpet—i.e. on the Last Day—people will be so terrified that they will be unable to call upon their relatives and others for help (23:101).

TRUST

Arabic: *tawakkul; amānah.*

I. Tawakkul.

1. *Meaning.* Tawakkul ("trust [in God]") is a virtue the Qur'ān seeks to inculcate in man. One should place one's trust in God alone (3:122, 159; 4:81; 5:11; 12:67; 14:11; 27:79; 33:3; 39:38), for He alone is Ever-Living (25:58), is Powerful (8:49; 12:67; 26:217), has control over everything (11:123), is Wise (8:49) and Merciful (26:217), and provides the right guidance (14:12). Placing one's trust in God is not only "expedient" for the above reasons, it is also one of the demands of faith (5:23; 10:84).

2. *Tawakkul and Fatalism.* To place one's complete trust in God is not tantamount to fatalism. In fact, one places one's trust in God in a matter only after doing all that is in one's power in regard to that matter. Jacob placed his complete trust in God (12:67) and is praised for that (12:68). And yet, before sending his sons to Egypt in search of Joseph, he asked them to take the necessary precautions. "My sons," he said, "do not enter by one door but enter by several different doors . . . Decision belongs to God alone; I have placed my trust in Him, and those who would place their trust should place it in Him alone" (12:67). Here, as can be seen, *tawakkul* is regarded as being complementary, and not antithetical, to planning and using one's judgment. The same lesson is taught by 3:159: "*Once you have made a resolve*, place your trust in God." That is, one should resort to *tawakkul* not before but after one has made the requisite effort he is supposed to make in regard to a matter.

II. Amānah.

1. *Two Meanings. Amānah* (pl. *amānāt*) has been used in the Qur'ān in a general and in a special sense, though the two will be found to be related. (The following treatment ignores the use of the word in 2:283, where *amānah* has the simple meaning of "article put in pledge.")

2. *General Use.* 4:58 commands Muslims "to hand over trusts to those to whom they belong." The word "trusts" here a very wide sense and refers to all responsibilities that devolve upon an individual, a group of people, or a nation, whether they are religious, ethical, legal, or political in nature. "To deliver *amānāt* to those to whom they belong" would cover, for example, the fulfilling of the agreement one has made with another individual, the discharging of one's duties to God, and the employing of one's faculties and capacities in a proper way. 8:27 forbids one to commit a breach of trust (*q.v.*), and 23:8 and 70:32 praise those who "keep their trusts." The use of the word *amānāt* in all these verses signifies that man will be held accountable by God for discharging his obligations.

3. *Special Use.* 33:72 says that God presented "The Trust" to the heavens and the earth but they refused to carry it, and that man agreed to carry it. Here *amānah* stands for voluntary obedience to God. In refusing to carry the *amānah*, the heavens and the earth refused to have the choice of obeying or disobeying God, and instead resigned to an "involuntary" worship of God. By agreeing to carry it, man chose to have the power to obey or disobey God. If, then, he offers obedience to God, he elevates himself to a status higher than that of angels (see *angel*) and makes himself deserving of a great reward. But if he disobeys Him, he descends to a level lower than that of beasts and justifies the infliction on him of great punishment. The *amānah* in the verse thus may be interpreted as destiny: in choosing to carry the *amānah*, man chose to be responsible for his destiny.

See also: BREACH OF TRUST; MAN.

TRUSTWORTHY SPIRIT, THE See HOLY SPIRIT, THE

TRUTH

Arabic: *ḥaqq*.

Ḥaqq, which has the general meaning of "truth," has a number of specific meanings in the Qur'ān:

1. That which is true, as a statement (6:73; 7:105), promise (10:55; 11:45; 14:22; 46:17), story (3:62), or dream (48:27). The Qur'ān is *ḥaqq* in this sense (2:26, 149; 5:84; 10:94; 13:1); Muḥammad presents the truth (2:119), and, since he represents the truth, is himself *ḥaqq* (3:86).

2. That which is correct and proper: when Moses explained to the Israelites what kind of cow they were supposed to slaughter, they said, "Now you have come up with the *ḥaqq*" (2:71).

3. That which is inevitable, as the Last Day (78:39).

4. True deity: God is thus called *ḥaqq* (6:62; 22:62; 31:30).

5. Justification: the Israelites killed prophets without *ḥaqq* (2:61; 3:21, 112, 181); no one may be put to death without *ḥaqq* (6:151).

6. Right due to someone (11:79; 17:26; 51:19; 70:24).

7. Obligation one must discharge (2:180, 241).

8. Purpose: God has created the universe with a definite purpose (6:73; 10:5; 14:19).

In the struggle between truth and falsehood (*q.v.*), the former will eventually triumph (7:118; 8:8).

See also: FALSEHOOD.

U

ULŪ L-AMR See AUTHORITY

UMM AL-KITĀB

The expression has been used in the Qur'ān in two senses:

1. "Mother Book," i.e. the Preserved Tablet (*q.v.*; 13:39; 43:4).

2. "Essential part of the Book," i.e. those Qur'ānic verses which are of fundamental importance (3:7). The "essential" or "fundamental" verses of the Qur'ān are the *muḥkamāt* (see *Qur'ān*).

See also: PRESERVED TABLET, THE; QUR'ĀN.

UMM AL-QURĀ See MOTHER CITY

UMMAH WASAṬ See MEDIAN COMMUNITY, THE

UMMĪ

Pagan Arabs, in contradistinction to the People of the Book (*q.v.*), lacked a scripture and were, generally, unacquainted with the arts of reading and writing, and so were called *ummiyyūn* (pl. of *ummī*, literally, "unlettered"). The term was originally used in a pejorative sense by the Israelites for Ishmaelites (3:75), but since the Ishmaelites were in fact "unlettered," the Qur'ān used the term for the Ishmaelites as a distinguishing mark (3:20; 62:2). In 7:157, 158 Muḥammad is called an *ummī* prophet (see *prophet*).

In 2:78 the word *ummiyyūn* refers to the illiterate among the Israelites.

ᶜUMRAH See PILGRIMAGE

UNLAWFUL, THE See LAWFUL AND THE UNLAWFUL, THE

UNSEEN, THE See FAITH; PHENOMENAL AND NON-PHENOMENAL REALMS, THE

ᶜURWAH AL-WUTHQĀ, AL- See FIRM HANDLE, THE

USWAH ḤASANAH See PROPHET

V

VERSE See ĀYAH

VICEGERENT See CALIPH

VISION See REVELATION

VOW

Arabic: *nadhr.*

To make a vow is to solemnly declare to do a good deed—like offering special prayers or giving charity—upon the fulfillment of a wish, prayer, plan, etc. A vow, once made, must be fulfilled (see 2:270; 22:29; 76:7).

The Qur'ān speaks of the vow made by the mother of Mary, who, hoping that she would give birth to a boy, dedicated the child to the service of God (3:35). According to 19:26, Mary, when she was pregnant with Jesus, made a vow to fast and remain silent during the fast (cf. "Be silent" in Zech. 2:13). As the verse indicates, she was instructed to do so by the angel who visited her.

W

WA'D See INFANTICIDE

WAḤY See REVELATION

WAITING PERIOD, THE

Arabic: *ᶜiddah.*

ᶜIddah is the period for which a woman who has received divorce must wait before the divorce becomes final and she is allowed to marry another man.

65:1 enjoins that the waiting period be carefully reckoned. This is in view of the importance of the waiting period, since the application of a number of religious injunctions depends on whether the period is completed.

The waiting period for a divorced woman is three monthly cycles (2:228); for a widow it is four months and ten days (2:234); for a pregnant woman the period extends to the birth of the child (65:4). A woman who has been divorced before the consummation of marriage does not have to observe the *ᶜiddah* (33:49).

During the waiting period the husband may not expel the wife from the house, unless she has committed gross immorality; the wife, too, must not leave the house (*q.v.*; 65:1). During the waiting period the husband has the right to take back the wife; the decision to take her back or divorce her finally must be made before the conclusion of the waiting period (2:228; 65:2). Whether the decision is to resume marriage or to divorce, two honest and reliable persons should be taken as witnesses (65:2). The husband is responsible for the maintenance of the wife during the waiting period (65:6).

See also: DIVORCE.

WALĀYAH

Walāyah literally means "support, friendship, guardianship." 8:72 uses the word in the sense of political and legal support. Referring to the migration (see *emigration*) of Muslims from Makkah to Madīnah, the verse says that the relationship of *walāyah* does not exist between the Madīnan Muslims and those Muslims who are still in Makkah and have not migrated. In other words, the bond of *walāyah* (as against the bond of brotherhood [*q.v.*]) exists only among Muslims who are residents of an Islamic State. The principle has legal and political implications, e.g. that an Islamic State will not be responsible for Muslims living in a non-Islamic State.

See also: BROTHERHOOD.

WAR See CIVIL WAR; JIHĀD

WARNER

Arabic: *mundhir, nadhīr.*

One of the major functions of a prophet (*q.v.*) is to warn his people (2:213; 4:165; 6:48; 18:56). He warns them of the grave consequences of rejecting the message he brings from God (6:130; 19:39; 34:46; 39:71; 40:15:42:7). God has raised a warner in every community (35:24), and He does not destroy nations without first sending warners to them (26:208).

Muḥammad is represented as being a warner to the Arabs (7:158; 11:2; 34:44) and to the whole mankind (25:1; 34:28); that is, he is a warner generally to mankind, especially to the Arabs.

See also: GIVER OF GOOD TIDINGS.

WAṢĪLAH See ANIMAL VENERATION

WAṢIYYAH See BEQUEST

WAYFARER

Arabic: *ibn as-sabīl.*

A "wayfarer" is a traveler. A person who is on a journey might need financial help even if he is otherwise a rich person. To receive such help is his right (17:26; 30:38), and to give such help is an act of virtue (2:177, 2:215; 4:36). Wayfarers are entitled to receive a share in *zakāt* (*q.v.*; 9:60) and *fay'* (see *spoils*; 59:7).

WELFARE DUE See ZAKĀT

WHITE STREAK, THE

Arabic: *al-khayṭ al-abyaḍ.*

2:187, speaking of fasting (*q.v.*), allows one to eat and drink during the night "until the white streak becomes distinct from the black streak for you." "The white streak" is the bright line seen in the horizon at daybreak which signals the end of the night and the beginning of the day. The fast begins at this time. The "black streak" (*al-khayṭ al-aswad*), unlike the white, is not a particular line in the horizon but represents the dark of the night as such, the expression being a rhetorical counterbalance to "the white streak."

WICKEDNESS See FISQ; FUJŪR

WINE AND GAME OF CHANCE

Arabic: *khamr* ("wine"); *maysir* ("game of chance").

I. Prohibition. 5:91 prohibits wine and games of chance, calling them weapons by means of which Satan (*q.v.*) creates hostility and rancor among people. In Arabia, gambling and wine-drinking had been responsible for some longstanding feuds, and even for wars that lasted for decades.

II. "Benefits" and "Sin." Before 5:91 categorically prohibited gambling and wine-drinking, 2:219 had stated that the two had certain "benefits," though their "sin" outweighed the benefits. What are the benefits the Qur'ān has in mind?

According to Iṣlāḥī, the Qur'ān is not referring to any medical and psychological benefits, but to the sociomoral benefits the Arabs associated with gambling and wine-drinking. In times of winter and drought, well-to-do Arabs got together, slaughtered animals, and drew lots to claim portions of the flesh. The portions won were then distributed among the poor and the needy, the act being looked upon as a great social service. The Qur'ān, then, is saying that the harm done by gambling and wine-drinking is so great that the presumed benefits are negligible. It is to be noted that the word "benefits" (*manāfi*^{c}) is opposed in the verse by "sin" (*ithm*), which is a moral category—another indication that social and moral rather than medical and psychological benefits are intended.

See also: DIVINATION; MAJOR SIN AND MINOR SIN.

WITNESS

Arabic: *shahādah*.

I. Literal Meaning. The literal meaning of *shahādah* is "presence." The phenomenal world is called the world of *shahādah* because it is "present" to our senses, and is to be contrasted with the world of *ghayb* (see *the phenomenal and non-phenomenal realms*).

II. Other Meanings. The literal meaning of *shahādah*, "presence," gives rise to the meaning "(to bear) testimony," which can be of several kinds (see below). The connection between "presence" and "testimony" is obvious: only one who is *present* on an occasion can *testify* as to what happened on that occasion.

The bearing of testimony (active participle: *shahīd* [pl. *shuhadā'*]) can take a number of forms, and the following meanings may be distinguished:

1. Bearing witness to an event (24:4, 6, 8, 13; 50:21).

2. Bearing witness to an agreement or transaction (2:282, 283; 5:106, 108).

3. Bearing witness to the truth of something, e.g. a divine message (2:143; 4:135; 5:44; 22:78; 57:19).

4. Representing or speaking for a group or people—a spokesman bears witness to the correctness of the stance or position of his people (2:23).

5. Keeping watch over something (3:98; 5:117; 10:46; 22:17).

6. Martyrdom—a martyr, by giving his life, bears witness to the truth of what he stands for (3:140). The martyrs, the Qur'ān says, are not dead, but are alive and are being provided sustenance by God (3:169).

WORLD, THE See EARTHLY LIFE

WORSHIP

Arabic: *ᶜibādah.*

ᶜIbādah means much more than "worship," the usual rendering. The literal meaning is "servanthood, slavehood," from which arises the technical meaning: an act of worship performed in obedience to God, in accordance with His command, and in order to seek His pleasure. On the ritualistic level, acts like *ṣalāt* (*q.v.*), *zakāt* (*q.v.*), fasting (*q.v.*), and pilgrimage (*q.v.*) may be called *ᶜibādah*. The Qur'ān, however, extends the concept of *ᶜibādah* to cover any act done in recognition of one's proper relationship with God, the relationship, that is, of a servant or slave to his master. In this sense, practically the whole of human life is brought under the rubric of *ᶜibādah*. 51:56 says that men (and the *jinn* [*q.v.*]) were created in order that they should serve and worship God.

ᶜIbādah is due only to God (9:31; 11:2; 12:40; 13:36; 17:23; 39:11), the Creator of the heavens and the earth (19:65). All prophets have called men to the worship of the One God (2:133; 11:2, 26; 41:14; 46:21). All beings and objects that are worshipped other than the One God are deities in name only, for there is no justification for their godhead (12:40), and they themselves have been created by God (7:194; 21:26; 43:19).

See also: ᶜABD; RABB.

WUḌŪ' See ABLUTION

Y

YAMĪN See OATH

YATĪM See ORPHAN

YAWM AD-DĪN See HEREAFTER, THE

YAM AL-FAṢL See HEREAFTER, THE

YAWM AL-FURQĀN See FURQĀN

YAWM AL-ḤAQQ, AL- See HEREAFTER, THE

YAWM AL-ḤISĀB See HEREAFTER, THE

YAWM AL-JAMᶜ See HEREAFTER, THE

YAWM AL-KHULŪD See HEREAFTER, THE

YAWM AL-KHURŪJ See HEREAFTER, THE

YAWM AL-MAWᶜŪD, AL- See HEREAFTER, THE

YAWM AL-QIYĀMAH See HEREAFTER, THE

YAWM AT-TAGHĀBUN See HEREAFTER, THE

YAWM AT-TALĀQĪ See HEREAFTER, THE

YAWM AT-TANĀDĪ See HEREAFTER, THE

YAWM AL-WA^{c}ĪD See HEREAFTER, THE

Z

ZAKĀT

I. Meaning. Muslims are required to pay *zakāt*. Literally "purity," *zakāt* is the technical name for the mandatory form of *ṣadaqah* (*q.v.*) Muslims have to pay. The details of *zakāt* and the conditions for its payment are taken from *Ḥadīth*. But since paying it is an obligation, *zakāt* may not be equated with charity, for the one who receives it is in no way beholden to the one who gives it. By paying *zakāt*, one meets an important obligation, thus "purifying" his wealth and his heart (hence the name *zakāt*) (9:103). Payment of *zakāt* is one of the conditions of salvation in the hereafter (23:4).

II. Importance. The Qur'ān presents *zakāt* as a religious obligation of longstanding origin. *Zakāt* did not originate with Islam, but was imposed by God on all nations before Islam (2:43, 83, 110; 19:31, 55; 21:73). The Qur'ān frequently mentions *zakāt* together with *ṣalāt* (*q.v.*; 2:43, 83, 110; 9:18, 71; 19:31, 55, 73; 22:78; 24:56; 27:3; 31:4; 58:13), implying that it is next only to *ṣalāt* in importance. The establishment of *ṣalāt* and payment of *zakāt* are described as the distinguishing marks of the Muslim community (9:11; also 9:5), and one of the distinguishing marks of righteous people is that, on achieving political power, they establish *ṣalāt* and pay *zakāt* (22:41; also 24:37). These verses make the establishment and management of the *zakāt* fund one of the fundamental responsibilities of an Islamic State.

III. Purpose and Function. *Zakāt* is aimed at preventing concentration of wealth and thus securing a more equitable distribution of wealth in society. The stated purpose of *fay'* (see *spoils*), "so that it [wealth] does not keep circulating among the rich ones of you" (59:7) is the purpose of *zakāt* also. As against interest (*q.v.*), which diminishes wealth, *zakāt* causes an increase in the amount of wealth (30:39). Complementing such other institutions as inheritance (see *inheritance, law of*), *zakāt* forms an important part of the Islamic economic system.

IV. Heads of Expenditure. The heads of expenditure of *zakāt* are given in 9:60, where the word *ṣadaqāt* (pl. of *ṣadaqah*) is used for *zakāt*. *Zakāt* funds are to be spent:

1. On the poor (*fuqarā'*; see *the needy*).

2. On the destitute (*masākīn*; see *the needy*).

3. On those engaged in the management of the *zakāt* fund (*al-ᶜāmilīna ᶜalayhā*; the salaries, etc., of these people will be paid out of the *zakāt* fund).

4. For the purpose of winning the goodwill and friendship of certain people (*al-mu'allafat qulūbuhum*), such as those opponents of Islam whom money can neutralize, or new converts, who, it is feared, will become apostates if not provided financial support. Such people may be given of the *zakāt* fund even if they are not poor or needy.

5. For the purpose of freeing slaves (*fī r-riqāb*).

6. On debtors (*al-ghārimīn*), that is, those who are so deep in debt that they are unable to meet subsistence requirements.

7. For the purpose of promoting Islam (*fī sabīl Allāh*, literally, "in the way of God"). This is a vast head and includes any and all measures taken to promote Islam.

8. On wayfarers (see *wayfarer*).

See also: INTEREST; ṢADAQAH; SPOILS.

ẒIHĀR See DIVORCE

ZINĀ See ADULTERY

ZĪNAH See DRESS

ẒULM SEE INIQUITY

LIST OF TERMS AND CONCEPTS

A

^{c}abd
ablution
ablution, dry *see* dry ablution
abrogation
accountability
accursed tree, the
^{c}adhāb *see* punishment
^{c}adl *see* justice
adultery
age of ignorance, the
^{c}ahd *see* covenant
ahl adh-dhikr *see* remembrance
ahl al-kitāb *see* people of the book, the
aḥzāb *see* confederates, the
ajal *see* appointed time, the
ākhirah *see* hereafter, the
Allāh
amānah *see* trust
amr bi l-ma^{c}rūf wa n-nahy ^{c}an al-munkar, al- *see* enjoining good and forbidding evil
ancient house, the
anfāl *see* spoils
angel

animal veneration
anṣāb *see* lawful and the unlawful, the
anṣār *see* helpers, the
apostasy
appointed time, the
arbitration
arḍ al-mubārakah, al- *see* blessed land, the
arḍ al-muqaddasah, al- *see* blessed land, the
ark of the covenant, the
^{c}arsh *see* throne
ascension
aṣḥāb al-mash'amah *see* deed-scroll
aṣḥāb al-maymanah *see* deed-scroll
aṣḥāb al-yamīn *see* deed-scroll
aṣḥāb ash-shimāl *see* deed-scroll
asmā' al-ḥusnā, al- *see* Allāh
atonement
authority
āyah
ayyām Allāh *see* days of God, the
azlām *see* divination

B

backbiting
baghy *see* dīn
bahīmat al-an^{c}ām *see* sacrifice
baḥīrah *see* animal veneration
balā' *see* trial
balance *see* mīzān
baldah al-muḥarramah, al- *see* sacred mosque, the
baptism *see* hue of God, the
barzakh
base desires *see* hawā
bashīr *see* giver of good tidings

bathing
bāṭil *see* falsehood
bay^{c}ah *see* oath of allegiance
bayt al-^{c}atīq, al- *see* ancient house, the
bayt al-ḥarām *see* sacred mosque, the
bayt al-muḥarram, al- *see* sacred house, the
bayyinah *see* manifest proof
belief *see* faith
bequest
bidding self, the
bighā' *see* compulsion
birr *see* piety
black streak, the *see* white streak, the
blasphemy
blessed land, the
blessing
blood *see* lawful and the unlawful, the
bloodwit
book *see* kitāb
breach of trust
brotherhood
bukhl *see* miserliness
burhān *see* manifest proof
burnt offering *see* sacrifice

C

caliph
censorious self, the
chance companion
charity *see* ṣadaqah.
chastity
chord of God, the
chord of people, the *see* chord of God, the
circumambulation *see* pilgrimage

civil war
companion, chance *see* chance companion
competition
compulsion
condescension
confederates, the
confidential talk *see* najwā
consultation, principle of
contented self, the
corruption
covenant
criterion, the
curse
customary law

D

ḍalāl *see* misguidance
ḍalālah *see* misguidance
day of judgment, the *see* hereafter, the
days of God, the
death
deed-scroll
dhikr *see* remembrance
dhikrā *see* remembrance
dīn
disbelief
disciple
discrimination between prophets
dissimulation
distant mosque, the
distortion of scripture
divination
divorce
diyah *see* bloodwit

double swearing
dower
dress
dry ablution
du^{c}ā' *see* prayer
dunyā *see* earthly life

E

earthly life
election
emigration
enjoining good and forbidding evil
envy
evil
extravagance

F

fāḥishah *see* immorality
faḥshā' *see* immorality
faith
falāḥ *see* salvation
false allegation of unchastity
falsehood
faqīr *see* needy, the
fasād *see* corruption
fasting
fawz *see* salvation
fay' *see* spoils
fidyah *see* atonement
fiqhting against God and His prophet
firdaws *see* heaven
firm handle, the

fisq
fitnah
fiṭrah
flogging
forgiveness
fornication *see* adultery
freedom and determinism
fujūr
furqān *see* criterion, the
fusūq *see* fisq

G

game of chance *see* wine and game of chance
ghanā'im *see* spoils
ghayb *see* phenomenal and non-phenomenal realms, the
ghībah *see* backbiting
ghusl *see* bathing
giver of good tidings
glorification of God
God *see* Allāh
good action
good loan
gratitude
greeting
guidance

H

ḥabl Allāh *see* chord of God, the
ḥabl an-nās *see* chord of God, the
ḥabṭ al-ᶜamal *see* nullification of deeds
ḥadīd *see* iron
hady *see* sacrifice; symbols of God

ḥajj *see* pilgrimage
ḥalf *see* oath
ḥallāf *see* oathmonger
ḥamd *see* gratitude
ḥāmī *see* animal veneration
ḥanīf
ḥaqq *see* truth
ḥāqqah *see* hour, the
ḥarām *see* sacred landmark, the; sacred months, the; sacred mosque, the; lawful and the unlawful, the
ḥasad *see* envy
ḥasanah *see* good action
hawā
ḥawārī *see* disciple
heaven
hell
helpers, the
hereafter, the
ḥibr
hijrah *see* emigration
ḥilf *see* oath
ḥisāb *see* accountability
holy land, the *see* blessed land, the
holy spirit, the
hour, the
hudā *see* guidance
ḥudūd Allāh *see* prescriptions of God
hue of God, the
ḥukm *see* arbitration
human nature *see* fiṭrah
hunting *see* atonement; lawful and the unlawful, the; pilgrimage
hypocrites, the

I

ᶜibādah *see* worship
Iblīs *see* Satan
ᶜiddah *see* waiting period, the
iḍlāl *see* misguidance
idolatry
iḍṭirār *see* necessity
iftidā' *see* divorce
ightisāl *see* bathing
ightiyāb *see* backbiting
ignorance, the age of *see* age of ignorance, the
iḥrām *see* pilgrimage
iḥsān *see* good action
iḥṣān *see* chastity; marriage
ikhfā' *see* distortion of scripture
ikhtiyān *see* breach of trust
ikhtiyār *see* election
īlā' *see* oath of sexual abstinence
ilḥād *see* blasphemy
īmān *see* faith
īmān bi l-ghayb *see* faith
imhāl *see* respite
imlā' *see* respite
immorality
impurity
infanticide
infāq *see* spending in the way of God
inheritance, law of
iniquity
insā' *see* abrogation
insān *see* man
inspiration *see* revelation
intercalation
intercession
interest

iqtiṣād *see* moderation
iron
irtidād *see* apostasy
ishrāk *see* idolatry
Islam
isrā' *see* ascension
isrāf *see* extravagance
iṣṭifā' *see* election
istikbār *see* pride
istiqsām bi l-azlām *see* divination
istiwa' ᶜalā l-ᶜarsh *see* throne
iᶜtikāf *see* fasting
izāghah *see* sealing

J

jahannam *see* hell
jāhiliyyah *see* age of ignorance, the
jald *see* flogging
jamᶜ bayn al-ukhtayn *see* marriage
jannah *see* heaven
jār al-junub, al- *see* neighbor
jār dhū l-qurbā, al- *see* neighbor
jazā' *see* recompense
jibt
jihād
jinn
justice

K

Kaᶜbah
kabīrah *see* major sin and minor sin
kaffārah *see* atonement

khalīfah *see* caliph
khamr *see* wine and game of chance
khātam an-nabiyyīn *see* seal of the prophets, the
khatm *see* sealing
khayṭ al-abyaḍ, al- *see* white streak, the
khayṭ al-aswad, al- *see* white streak, the
khiyānah *see* breach of trust
khul^{c} *see* divorce
kitāb
kufr *see* disbelief
kursī *see* throne

L

la^{c}nah *see* curse
law of inheritance *see* inheritance, law of
lawful and the unlawful, the
lawḥ maḥfūẓ *see* preserved tablet, the
laylat al-qadr *see* night of decree, the
layy *see* distortion of scripture
lesser pilgrimage, the *see* pilgrimage
li^{c}ān *see* double swearing
libās *see* dress

M

maghfirah *see* forgiveness
magic
maḥrūm *see* needy, the
major sin and minor sin
malak *see* angel
man
manifest proof
mann *see* condescension

mann and salwā
mansak *see* sacrifice
marriage
martyrdom *see* witness
ma^{c}rūf *see* customary law; enjoining good and forbidding evil
mash^{c}ar al-ḥarām, al- *see* sacred landmark, the
masjid al-aqṣā, al- *see* distant mosque, the
masjid al-ḥarām, al- *see* sacred mosque, the
mawqūdhah *see* lawful and the unlawful, the
mawt *see* death
maysir *see* wine and game of chance
median community, the
median path, the *see* median community, the; right path, the
messenger *see* prophet
milk al-yamīn *see* slavery
minor sin *see* major sin and minor sin
miracle
miserliness
misguidance
miskīn *see* needy, the
mīthāq *see* covenant
mīzān
moderation
monk *see* monasticism
monasticism
monotheism
mother city
mu'allafat al-qulūb *see* zakāt
mubashshir *see* giver of good tidings
mubāya^{c}ah *see* oath of allegiance
muhājarah *see* emigration
muḥārabah *see* fighting against God and His prophet
muhaymin *see* Qur'ān
muḥkamāt *see* Qur'ān

mukātabah *see* slavery
munāfiq *see* hypocrites, the
mundhir *see* warner
munkar *see* enjoining good and forbidding evil
munkhaniqah *see* lawful and the unlawful, the
musābaqah *see* competition
Muslim *see* dīn; Islam
mutaraddiyah *see* lawful and the unlawful, the
mutashābihāt *see* Qur'ān
mutual cursing *see* double swearing

N

nabī *see* prophet
nadhīr *see* warner
nadhr *see* vow
nafs al-ammārah, an- *see* bidding self, the
nafs al-lawwāmah *see* censorious self, the
nafs al-muṭma'innah, an- *see* contented self, the
najwā
nasī' *see* intercalation
naskh *see* abrogation
naṭīḥah *see* lawful and the unlawful, the
nature
nature, human *see* fiṭrah
necessity
needy, the
neighbor
night of decree, the
nikāḥ *see* marriage
nullification of deeds
nushūz
nuṣub *see* lawful and the unlawful, the
nusuk *see* sacrifice

O

oath
oath of allegiance
oath of sexual abstinence *see* īlā'
oathmonger
original sin, the *see* forgivenss; man; repentance
orphan
ostentation

P

paradise *see* heaven
people of the book, the
persecution *see* fitnah
perseverance
phenomenal and non-phenomenal realms, the
piety
pilgrimage
polygyny *see* marriage
polytheism *see* idolatry
prayer
prayer, ritual *see* ṣalāt
predestination *see* freedom and determinism
prescriptions of God
preserved tablet, the
pride
proof, manifest *see* manifest proof
prophecy
prophet
prostitution *see* compulsion
providence *see* rabb
punishment

Q

qadhf *see* false allegation of unchastity
qalā'id *see* symbols of God
qarḍ ḥasan *see* good loan
qasam *see* oath
qaṣd *see* moderation
qiblah
qiṣāṣ
qissīs
qisṭ *see* justice
qitāl *see* jihād
Qur'ān
qurbān *see* sacrifice

R

rabb
rabbānī
raḍā^{c}ah *see* suckling
rahbāniyyah *see* monasticism
rāhib *see* monasticism
Ramaḍān
ramy *see* false allegation of unchastity
rasūl *see* prophet
recompense
religion *see* dīn
remembrance
repentance
respite
resurrection *see* hereafter, the; hour, the
retaliation *see* qiṣāṣ
revelation
reward
ribā *see* interest

ribbī *see* rabbānī
right path, the
righteouness *see* piety
risālah *see* prophecy
ritual prayer *see* ṣalāt
rūḥ *see* holy spirit, the; revelation
rūḥ al-amīn ar- *see* holy spirit, the
rūḥ al-qudus, ar- *see* holy spirit, the
ru'yā' *see* ascension; revelation

S

sā^c^ah *see* hour, the
Sabeans
ṣabr *see* perseverance
sacred house, the *see* sacred mosque, the
sacred land, the *see* sacred mosque, the
sacred landmark, the
sacred months, the
sacred mosque, the
sacrifice
ṣadaqah
ṣaduqah *see* dower
ṣaghīrah *see* major sin and minor sins
ṣāḥib bi l-janb, aṣ- *see* chance companion
sā'ibah *see* animal veneration
sā'il *see* needy, the
salām *see* greeting
ṣalāt
ṣalāt al-fajr *see* ṣalāt
ṣalāt al-^c^ishā' *see* ṣalāt
ṣalāt al-wusṭā, aṣ- *see* ṣalāt
ṣalāt at-tahajjud *see* ṣalāt
ṣāliḥ *see* good action
salvation

salwā *see* mann and salwā

sanctuary of peace, the

sariqah *see* theft

Satan

sawā' as-sabīl *see* median community, the

ṣawm *see* fasting

scales, the *see* mīzān

scripture *see* kitāb

seal of the prophets, the

sealing

sha^{c}ā'ir Allāh *see* symbols of God

shafā^{c}ah *see* intercession

shahādah *see* phenomenal and non-phenomenal realms, the; witness

shahīd *see* witness

shahr al-ḥarām, ash- *see* sacred months, the

shajarah al-mal^{c}ūnah, ash- *see* accursed tree, the

sharr *see* evil

shayṭān *see* Satan

shirk *see* idolatry

shukr *see* gratitude

shūrā *see* consultation, principle of

ṣibghat Allāh *see* hue of God, the

siḥr *see* magic

sin *see* major sin and minor sin

ṣirāṭ al-mustaqīm, al- *see* right path, the

ṣiyām *see* fasting

slavery

sorcery *see* magic

spending in the way of God

spirit *see* holy spirit, the; revelation

spoils

suckling

sulṭān *see* manifest proof

sunnah of God

superstition *see* animal veneration; divination; jibt

ṣūr *see* trumpet, the
symbols of God

T

ṭab^{c} *see* sealing
tabarruj *see* ostentation
tabdhīr *see* extravagance
tadhkirah *see* remembrance
tadhkiyah *see* lawful and the unlawful, the
tābūt *see* ark of the covenant, the
tafrīq bayn ar-rusul *see* discrimination between prophets
ṭāghūt
taḥlīl *see* lawful and the unlawful, the
taḥrīf *see* distortion of scripture
taḥrīm *see* lawful and the unlawful, the
takabbur *see* pride
takāthur *see* competition
ṭalāq *see* divorce
tanājī *see* najwā
taqdīs *see* glorification of God
taqiyyah *see* dissimulation
taqwā *see* piety
tasbīḥ *see* glorification of God
taṣdīq *see* Qur'ān
taskhīr *see* nature
ṭaṣrīf *see* Qur'ān
tawakkul *see* trust
tawbah *see* repentance
tawbah naṣūḥ *see* repentance
tawḥīd *see* monotheism
tayammum *see* dry ablution
ṭaysīr *see* freedom and determinism; Qur'ān
testimony *see* witness
thawāb *see* reward

theft
throne
trial
trumpet, the
trust
trustworthy spirit, the *see* holy spirit, the
truth *see* ḥaqq

U

ukhuwwah *see* brotherhood
ᶜukūf *see* fasting
ulū l-amr *see* authority
umm al-kitāb
umm al-qurā *see* mother city
ummah wasaṭ *see* median community, the
ummī
ᶜumrah *see* pilgrimage
unlawful, the *see* lawful and the unlawful, the
unseen, the *see* faith; phenomenal and non-phenomenal realms, the
ᶜurwah al-wuthqā, al- *see* firm handle, the
uswah ḥasanah *see* prophet

V

verse *see* āyah
vicegerent *see* caliph
vision *see* revelation
vow

W

wa'd *see* infanticide
waḥy *see* revelation
waiting period, the
walāyah
war *see* civil war; jihād
warner
waṣīlah *see* animal veneration
waṣiyyah *see* bequest
wayfarer
welfare due *see* zakāt
white streak, the
wickedness *see* fisq; fujūr
wine and game of chance
witness
world, the *see* earthly life
worship
wuḍū' *see* ablution

Y

yamīn *see* oath
yatīm *see* orphan
yawm ad-dīn *see* hereafter, the
yawm al-faṣl *see* hereafter, the
yawm al-furqān *see* criterion, the
yawm al-ḥaqq, al- *see* hereafter, the
yawm al-ḥisāb *see* hereafter, the
yawm al-jam^{c} *see* hereafter, the
yawm al-khulūd *see* hereafter, the
yawm al-khurūj *see* hereafter, the
yawm al-maw^{c}**ūd, al-** *see* hereafter, the
yawm al-qiyāmah *see* hereafter, the
yawm at-taghābun *see* hereafter, the

yawm at-talāqī *see* hereafter, the
yawm at-tanādī *see* hereafter, the
yawm al-wa^{c}īd *see* hereafter, the

Z

zakāt
ẓihār *see* divorce
zinā *see* adultery
zīnah *see* dress
ẓulm *see* iniquity